1965

This book may be kep

FOUR

charged

University of St. Francis
GEN 724.1 L919
Lowry
Renaissance architecture

3 0301 00023599 0

724.1
L919

36449

W9-ABR-680

RENAISSANCE ARCHITECTURE

THE GREAT AGES OF WORLD ARCHITECTURE

GREEK   *Robert L. Scranton*
ROMAN   *Frank E. Brown*
EARLY CHRISTIAN AND BYZANTINE   *William L. MacDonald*
MEDIEVAL   *Howard Saalman*
GOTHIC   *Robert Branner*
RENAISSANCE   *Bates Lowry*
BAROQUE AND ROCOCO   *Henry A. Millon*
MODERN   *Vincent Scully Jr.*

In Preparation
PERSIAN   *Arthur Upham Pope*
CHINESE AND INDIAN   *Nelson Wu*
PRE-COLUMBIAN   *Donald Robertson*
WESTERN ISLAMIC   *John Hoag*
JAPANESE

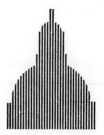

RENAISSANCE ARCHITECTURE

by Bates Lowry

LIBRARY
College of St. Francis
JOLIET, ILL.

PRENTICE-HALL INTERNATIONAL · LONDON

GEORGE BRAZILLER, INC. · NEW YORK

To my Mother

All rights in this book are reserved.
Published simultaneously in 1962 in New York by
George Braziller, Inc.
and in London, England by
Prentice-Hall International, Inc.
28 Welbeck Street, London W. 1

Printed in the Netherlands

724.1
£919

CONTENTS

36449

CHAPTER ONE

When around 1465 the Duke of Urbino, Federico da Monte-feltro, undertook to build a new palace, he believed only one kind of architect could design for him a building of such beauty that it would reflect and perpetuate the fame of his deeds. The man the Duke hoped to discover was one who practiced the art of building in the same manner as the architects of classical Rome. To find the person who had been "initiated into the mystery of this art" through a study and an appreciation of the works of the classical past, the Duke was forced to search throughout Italy, for the style he preferred above all others had only recently been brought back to architecture.[1]

One architect who would have been delighted to be chosen by the Duke of Urbino was Filarete, a Florentine architect whose own patron, the ruler of Milan, Duke Francesco Sforza, was not as fully convinced of the superiority of this manner of building. To sway the Sforza ruler over to the cause of this new kind of architecture, Filarete wrote in the 1460's a book describing the virtues of the classical style and urging its adoption in place of the one presently followed–the medieval style, which Filarete describes as having been "brought into Italy by the barbarians." Some thirty or forty years ago, he writes, the style of the ancients had been revived and now its superiority was recognized by all discerning men.[2] As members of this group, both Filarete and the Duke of Urbino shared a belief that their own era had seen an important change occur in the ideals that architects strove to achieve in their buildings. The standards of the medieval architects seemed to them to have been discarded by a few contemporary architects in favor of more desirable aesthetic values that were taken from works of the more distant classical past.

This concept of the 1460's about the origin and nature of "good" contemporary architecture–the style of architecture which we call "Renaissance"–was developed by men like the Duke of Urbino and Filarete primarily as a result of the work of only two men: Brunelleschi (1377–1446) and Alberti (1404–1472). It was in Tuscany, the area surrounding Brunelleschi's native city of Florence, where the Duke first looked for an architect because, as he says, it was the "fountainhead" of such men. Filarete refers specifically to Brunelleschi's work in Florence as marking the revival of the ancient style, and he mentions a work by Alberti as a recent example of the new manner of building. In fact, during the years prior to 1450, Brunelleschi was the sole architect in Italy whose buildings might be taken to indicate a new kind of architecture. After Brunelleschi's death in 1446, Alberti began to work as an architect and for approximately the next twenty years the "rebirth" of classical architecture was continued and directed principally by him. Of these two men, Brunelleschi is the "inventor," the artist to whose vision are due works of art conceived in a distinctly different manner from those of his predecessors. Alberti is the "critic," the interpreter whose writings and own buildings established the works of Brunelleschi as the foundation of a new style. Together they formulated a new attitude toward the creation of a work of architecture which not only determined the opinions voiced by discerning men of the 1460's, but which ultimately directed the basic approach of all Renaissance architects.

In the history of architecture this new attitude makes a startling appearance, for it seems to begin without the preliminary gropings or tentative thrusts toward a complete statement of principles that normally accompany a fundamental change in style. The first approach distinctly different from that of the medieval architect occurs in a work whose every detail is governed by this new attitude—Brunelleschi's design of 1419 for the Foundling Hospital in Florence (plate 1). Its graceful series of round arches and its flat, delicately articulated upper-wall rose within the darker, more massive medieval stone buildings of Florence as a completely new architectural statement. To Brunelleschi's contemporaries, the Hospital façade must have presented a vision as exciting as the one created in the early 1950's by the sight of the shimmering glass box of the Lever House set amid the dark stone buildings of New York's Park Avenue. But unlike the New York building, the Foundling Hospital had no forerunners either in actual or ideal structures, and for approximately the next twenty-five years it remained the only building of its kind to be seen within the streets of Florence. As such it was the principal work whose visual appearance could be the basis for the belief of those men—Alberti as well as others—that a rebirth of classical style had occurred in their time.

The Florentine spectator would have found at least two qualities in the Hospital façade that set it apart from other, recently constructed buildings.[3] On the one hand, he must have been surprised to discover architectural elements—round arches, Corinthian capitals, columns, pilasters, and window pediments —elements he was accustomed to see only in buildings he knew as examples of an ancient architectural style (plates 3, 4). Even more striking, however, must have been the unusual and inexplicable sensation received from being able to comprehend this building more completely and more immediately than any other one he had seen. The impression gained from a building like Brunelleschi's—one in which the effect of any one part is subordinated to the effect of the whole—would have been a very novel experience for a spectator accustomed to having his impression of a building stem mainly from the appearance and effect of its separate parts. Unlike his experience with a richly-decorated Gothic building like Or San Michele, the spectator confronted by the Hospital façade was not distracted from the whole by sinuous ornaments which seduced his eye into making aimless, pleasurable movements. Nor, as would have been his experience with the enormous, overwhelming structure of the

11

Loggia dei Lanzi, was the natural acuity of his eye blurred by seeing architectural elements so vastly scaled that they distended his field of vision. Instead, the architectonic rigor with which Brunelleschi handled ornamental details, the uniform scaling of each part of the building, as well as their consistently clear and precise delineation, sharpened the impact already made by the sight of a building composed of a series of identical units. The spectator had the sense of comprehending the whole of this building because its appearance encouraged him to believe that he could see, beneath the surface, the design that was responsible both for its form and for his own experience of it.

The spectator's startlingly clear impression of the Hospital façade, moreover, stimulated in him not only a feeling of being able to perceive the design responsible for the building's appearance, but also an awareness of the man responsible for the design. A similar awareness might have been provoked by the sight of any one of the many buildings constructed in Florence according to the orderly, precise art of the medieval master-mason. In these instances, however, the spectator was more likely to be conscious of the craftsman whose strength and skill had positioned and carved the stones, than to be aware, as he was with Brunelleschi's building, of the man whose mind had determined the entire design.

This aspect of the contemporary observer's experience with the Hospital façade would have been unique, even if he had been one of the uncommon few who had seen one of the medieval mason's most impressive accomplishments, the one that most clearly conveyed a sense of an underlying design—the French Gothic cathedral. A view along the interior nave wall of Chartres, Amiens, or Bourges—a sight, incidentally, that Brunelleschi certainly would have enjoyed—could not have failed to give such a spectator the clear impression of being within a geometrically ordered world. But because its visual design could not easily have been comprehended in its entirety, the French cathedral denied the spectator any sense that would enable him to determine exactly how this order was achieved. He would have been more likely to see the science of geometry itself as the force that determined the appearance of the building, rather than to be aware of the man who had used its principles to construct the edifice. That the opposite was true for the spectator's experience of the Hospital façade resulted from the fact that his sensation of being able to grasp the totality of this building at the first moment of perception created for him the illusion of being capable of determining precisely how the order he sensed had been achieved. Brunelleschi's building presented a visual image that was not merely suggestive of geometry, but one which had the rigor and clarity of a geometrical construction set forth as proof of a theorem.

As a result of these varied, new sensations, the spectator must have felt a force and fascination exerted by the first of Brunelleschi's buildings that made it a special object within his experience. The contact he felt capable of establishing with this object was one which he must have recognized as having a counterpart only in another, equally recent and novel experience with a work of art—his first view of a painting constructed according to the newly invented laws of perspective.[4] Like the clearly delineated parts of the Hospital façade, each of the objects in the painting was seen within a context established by the whole design. Within the frame of the painting existed an ordered world, the measurable space of which was occupied by objects whose size was relative to one another and to their position in depth. A glimpse of this lucid and comprehensible arrangement of objects behind the picture frame must have reminded the spectator of the sight of the arches, columns, and windows of the Hospital façade set within the precisely defined frame of the steps, side pilasters, and cornice. Either object would have generated the same feeling of the ability to grasp and comprehend a visual image in such an immediate and complete manner that its reality as a work of art or an object to be experienced was heightened. Although the method of producing this illusion was different in each work, both such a painting and the building by Brunelleschi were created according to the same principles because their intended effect was the same—the presentation of a visual image whose total form was dictated by a concern for how it would appear to the eye of the human observer.

The perspective system which the painter had chosen to be the means of controlling the relationship between his work and the observer was a particular application of results stemming from discoveries made by both Brunelleschi and Alberti.[5] For perspective was an invention that had emerged out of the desire of both these men to be able to determine the actual structure of an object from its visual appearance. Brunelleschi's desire most probably was rooted in a practical concern to record

13

accurately the physical structure of classical ruins—to make scale drawings. Only by this means, hitherto unknown, could he wrest from these buildings the secrets of construction that his fifteenth-century biographer, Manetti,[6] tells us was his purpose in excavating and measuring the ancient ruins. In part, Alberti's investigations were conducted out of a similar desire to record faithfully the remains of the classical buildings; he invented an instrument for doing so and later wrote on the methods of measuring and surveying. Each of these men transferred his invention from an immediate practical application into a pictorial one, for both demonstrated their discoveries in paintings. Alberti chose to represent seascapes (probably because of their "natural" horizon line), while Brunelleschi represented a part of the city of Florence which his viewers would have frequented daily.[7] In this dramatic way, Brunelleschi and Alberti demonstrated a means by which the artist could control the transfer of a desired mental image into physical form, and thus made possible the realization of an approach toward the creation of a work of art which was fundamentally different from that of the medieval period. For the use of the perspective system in painting was only a symbol of an attitude toward the creative act which placed a premium on the work of art as a product of the mind of man. By this attitude, the artist no longer was judged as a skilled manipulator of physical material but as a creator of mental images that could be interpreted by the observer in the philosophical terms of beauty and truth.

In the Foundling Hospital, this approach toward the creation of a work of architecture produced for the spectator an aesthetic experience that men like the Duke of Urbino or Filarete would interpret as signifying a rebirth of the classical style. Naturally, the unusual presence of antique elements in the contemporary façade of the Foundling Hospital could in itself suggest an association between Brunelleschi's work and that of the classical past. However, the mere existence of such elements could not alone give rise to a belief like Filarete's that the Foundling Hospital was a reincarnation of a classical building. Instead, this view was the result of the context in which the classical elements were presented. It was the combined effect of a completely new architectural statement, made in a recognizably older language of visual forms, that produced the very special reaction of the classically-minded spectator. For him, seeing Brunelleschi's building was an experience that enabled him to perceive how the now time-worn, half-ruined buildings of antiquity had appeared when newly built. "I appear to be re-born" is how one observer, described by Filarete, interpreted his experience of a building like the Foundling Hospital. When he looked at such buildings, this observer said, he believed he could see in them the buildings that, from his reading, he knew to have existed in ancient Rome and Egypt.[8] Thus, by the humanists, the visual image of Brunelleschi's building was invested with a particular meaning.

If the humanists interpreted the visual appearance of the Foundling Hospital as fulfilling their concept of what a classical building—Roman or Egyptian—*should* look like, this concept itself had not been formed primarily from visual evidence. Even their concept of the original state of Roman buildings close at hand was necessarily a literary one, since none of these works had survived in an unaltered state. This literary image itself did not come only from the fragmentary descriptions of antique buildings scattered through the classical texts, but was a result of their entire humanistic training. The development of a sensitivity to the established artistic forms in which an oration, poem or letter was presented, as well as a feeling for the form of the language itself was a goal of the humanist's study equal in importance to a knowledge and understanding of classical authors. All of their studies encouraged the humanists to develop a critical sense in which the ability to perceive form was the primary basis for qualitative judgment. From his acquired familiarity with ideal forms—the orations of Cicero, the epic poem of Virgil, or the letters of Pliny—the humanist was led to seek the same qualities in other works. His appreciation of artistic form as the expressive vehicle of the individual creative artist transferred itself from a purely literary phenomenon into a general aesthetic attitude—a transfer reflected in Filarete's statement that "the man who follows the ancient practice in architecture does exactly the same thing as the man of letters who strives to reproduce the classical style of Cicero and Virgil."[9] In a building like the Foundling Hospital the humanists were for the first time able to perceive in visual form the same standards they had learned to appreciate by studying classical literature. The same lucidity of form shone through the works of both Brunelleschi and the classical authors.

At the time the Foundling Hospital was begun, an appreciation of the sense of form displayed in the works of the classical authors had been developing in Italy for the past one hundred years. Starting in the fourteenth century with Petrarch, scholars had become increasingly desirous of studying the classics in their original state rather than in the formulations given to them by later commentators. Their interest was aroused not merely by the knowledge to be found in the classical writings but by the form in which the authors presented it. In the visual arts, this increased appreciation of formal artistic qualities was expressed by an admiration for classical works of art that acclaimed them for their own sake rather than for their power to evoke historical associations. The artists of the 1370's were stunned by the craftsmanship displayed in the ancient works of art. One artist described his feeling for them by saying "that if they but had a spark of life they would be better than Nature" and that their creators "had not just imitated Nature but indeed had excelled it."[10] Although primarily appreciative of the Roman works of art for their artistic quality rather than for their value as reminders of the past, these men nevertheless were conscious of them as objects that came from a distant time more glorious than their own. Their delight and amazement was tinged with regret for they did not believe it still possible for such works to be created. These works had been produced by men whose abilities could no longer be matched, men whom the artists of the present could not possibly hope to emulate.

Brunelleschi and other Florentine artists of the early fifteenth century shared in the existing enthusiasm for the works of the classical past, but not in the attitude that works of such quality could no longer be created. This view ended abruptly with the vigorous activity in the arts which took place in Florence at that time. Suddenly men seemed able to create works of a beauty that paralleled the ancients'. Partially, this resulted simply from the fact that the artists during the previous period had worked in such a way that formal qualities became increasingly important. But basically this change took place because artists like Brunelleschi or Donatello set out to discover the principles which the classical artists had followed when creating works that seemed so beautiful. What they discovered, or imagined they had discovered, they sought to use in their own work. As they did so, they dispelled the myth that the ancient talents were no longer to be found and, at least in one case—Alberti's—initiated the belief that in their time a classical reawakening was in the process of occurring. Alberti chooses to describe the impact of seeing the work of these Florentine artists for the first time in terms of just such a change of attitude.[11] Previously, he writes, he had been perplexed that so many of the arts and sciences he read about in classical literature seemed in his time to have almost entirely disappeared. But, after coming to Florence and seeing what her artists were able to create, particularly the buildings of Brunelleschi and the sculpture of Donatello, Alberti discarded this pessimistic opinion. Here, in Florence, he had found proof that in his time there existed men of such genius that their works of art could rival those of ancient Rome.

Alberti's admiration for the works of art he discovered on visiting Florence in 1434 probably was heightened by his friendship, already formed in Rome, with at least two of the artists—Brunelleschi and Donatello. But the nature of their works alone was bound to create a tremendous impact upon him as they fulfilled, and in some instances probably inspired, the concept Alberti had begun to formulate of the ideal work of art. Seeing the statues by Ghiberti and Donatello at Or San Michele,[12] Alberti could not help but be enthusiastic over finding himself in the presence of the first, large-size, bronze statues cast since antiquity. And surely he felt a special thrill of delight upon seeing Donatello's bronze *David*, his first view of a free-standing, nude statue, so like those he had read about.[13] And, how sharp his excitement must have been when shown the *Trinity* fresco by Masaccio,[14] where he could see for the first time the application on a large scale of the same principles of perspective with which he, too, had been experimenting. Every day Alberti must have discovered other works of art in which he saw realized by men of his own time the ideals he had become committed to primarily from an experience of the works of classical artists and writers.

The sense of personal achievement that was so basic in Alberti's admiration of these works could nowhere be more aroused than by the work of Brunelleschi. Although at the time of his visit few of Brunelleschi's buildings were completed, Alberti could not help but be amazed at the number and size of the projects begun, each of which presented to him another example of Brunelleschi's new approach to architecture. Alberti must have been taken from one project to another to see the work in progress or to examine the wooden models and designs Brunelleschi had prepared for the buildings. Entering the medieval cloister of S. Croce, for example, he would have seen, rising at the far end, the Pazzi Chapel (plate 17)—a small structure

17

which, in its half-finished state, must have appeared much like a ruined antique temple. Of its present interior (plates 20, 21), Alberti probably only knew the designs, but he could anticipate its effect to some extent when visiting the church of S. Lorenzo as its sacristy (designed 1418, completed 1428) was essentially an earlier version by Brunelleschi of the Pazzi interior design. Standing within the space so precisely confined by the white walls and the darker, articulating elements, Alberti must have considered the clarity with which the basic forms of the building are presented to have been the result of a process as inescapably correct as the reasoning of a logician.

Yet, no matter what project Alberti visited, he was constantly in the shade of Brunelleschi's still more impressive achievement—the dome of the Cathedral (plate 2). In 1434, the dome, nearly completed after fourteen years of work, stood as a monument to the creative genius of its designer. By his study of the Roman ruins and through his own intellect, Brunelleschi had succeeded where the guild of masons, whose "secrets of construction" previously had enabled them to erect all the major Florentine buildings, had failed. Not only had Brunelleschi constructed the dome according to methods of his own invention, but he did so in a manner that awed his contemporaries because it seemed to defy the natural laws of gravity. That the entire mass of stone overhanging a void about three hundred and fifty feet wide and three hundred feet high had been laid without the support of a massive wooden trusswork, was a sensational demonstration of Brunelleschi's ingenuity. Of all this, and probably also of Brunelleschi's struggle to have his ideas adopted, Alberti must have been keenly aware as he watched the over two hundred men work to complete the task under Brunelleschi's supervision. His admiration could only continue to mount as he watched in operation the hoisting machine invented twelve years earlier by Brunelleschi and which still was in use after having raised up over twenty-five thousand tons of the material needed to erect the dome.

When Alberti climbed to the top of the dome, for surely a man of his enquiring mind would not have been content only to look at the structure from below, Brunelleschi probably pointed out to him his plans for completely redesigning one section of the city across the Arno in order to create a proper setting for his new church of S. Spirito[15] (plates 8, 9, 11). Here they also probably discussed Brunelleschi's designs for the lantern which was to crown the dome. But the most amazing and impressive sight Alberti could have seen from atop the dome was the plan outlined by the rising foundations of S. Maria degli Angeli (plates 22, 23). The newest of Brunelleschi's buildings, this chapel-ringed, centrally planned, church must have looked to Alberti like the excavated remains of a Roman tomb. It was to him the clearest proof that with Brunelleschi the ancient style of architecture had been reborn.

When Alberti's visit to Florence from 1434–36 came to an end,[16] he must have left with the firm conviction not only that men of genius again worked in the creative arts, but that the presence or absence of this superiority was directly related to the degree in which these artists' works were related to the antique ones. This latter belief of Alberti was responsible for channeling into a single direction the new attitude toward the creation of a work of art—a direction in which it was to move for approximately the next one hundred and fifty years. From now on, the architect's approach to his work was to be characterized by a self-conscious desire to recreate the appearance of classical buildings.

If Alberti interpreted Brunelleschi's architectural innovations and achievements as a revival of classical art, he also appears to have recognized that Brunelleschi had not deliberately set out to recreate the external forms of this art, for within his praise of this architect he specifically commented that Brunelleschi's work had been accomplished without following the example of any earlier models. The evidence of the buildings themselves, if not the oral statements of their designer, would have convinced Alberti that Brunelleschi's motivation was different from his own. Thus, although in their unfinished state Brunelleschi's buildings may have appeared like classical ruins, Alberti, nevertheless, would have noted that their over-all design had little or no relationship to classical models. Rather than stemming from clearly identifiable monuments of the ancient past, Brunelleschi's designs were more specifically linked to a traditional style of a more recent time. With the exception of the centrally planned church of S. Maria degli Angeli (plates 22, 23), Brunelleschi adopted only fragments from antique architecture, like the columns and pilasters at S. Lorenzo (plates 3–5), and placed them within general compositional schemes that had their closest counterparts in the Romanesque buildings of Tuscany or in early Christian basilicas. The columnar naves of either S. Lorenzo or S. Spirito (plates 5, 9), for example, are echoes of churches like SS. Apostoli in Florence (plate 10) or like the basilicas of Rome and Ravenna. Even the temple-like façade of the Pazzi Chapel seems to owe its compositional design to the original nave elevation of St. Peter's basilica in Rome (plates 17, 18). That these buildings should have appeared to the humanists like classical buildings—reborn—was primarily the result of Brunelleschi's desire to create a building of whose form the spectator would be particularly conscious. This humanistic interpretation of the visual image of these buildings was now set forth by Alberti as the ideal of the architecture of his time—the same ideal that the Duke of Urbino sought for his palace and that Filarete sought to establish in the mind of his patron.

CHAPTER TWO

Shortly after Brunelleschi's death in 1446, Alberti began to put his ideal of architecture into material form by following closely the model provided both by the Roman ruins and by the writings of Vitruvius, the only existing classical treatise on architecture.[17] His approach to the creation of a work of architecture was a natural extension of the general concept Alberti held about the nature of a work of art. Any work of art was envisaged by Alberti principally as an object to be judged in terms of its relationship to a model taken either from the world of Nature or from the work of her most accomplished interpreters—the artists of the classical era. Although the latter was preferable, as antique works were ideal distillations of the best qualities of Nature, in either instance, Alberti sought the creation of an image—painted, sculptural, or architectural—that would be as "lifelike" or perfect a rendition of the model as possible.

Guided by this precept, Alberti already had written in 1434 his book of instructions for painters in which he described the geometrical principles underlying his invention of perspective. Now, probably during the years shortly after his return to Rome in 1443, Alberti began to write a more ambitious work—a book on the art of building.[18] In emulation of his classical model—the treatise by Vitruvius—Alberti divided his text into ten books, although neither the contents within each book nor the organization of the material is the same as Vitruvius'. That some other form might have been preferable because of a logical structure inherent in the material of the completed book (after Book V the division into books becomes increasingly arbitrary) apparently was not, in Alberti's opinion, sufficient reason to forego giving to his treatise the outward form of its classical model. A similar attitude governs Alberti's approach to his buildings.

Alberti's first building rose not far away from the Foundling Hospital by Brunelleschi. Begun during the period 1446–50, the Palazzo Rucellai (plates 15, 16) presented to the Florentine observer his first view of a building whose design was the result of a conscious attempt to recreate the appearance of a classical building. Not only does every detail of the façade have an antique prototype—except the division into two smaller units of the large, round-arched window openings—but they occur within an overall design that in itself seems to derive from a classical model. The pilasters, friezes, and cornices of Alberti's building are seen within what appears to be their natural or proper setting—a condition brought about primarily by the fact that the wall surface between them was designed to suggest an antique method of laying masonry. The classical motifs, which in Brunelleschi's buildings are apt to be read as "quotations" because they are so precisely set off from the wall surface itself, become in Alberti's work indistinguishable parts of the "body" of the façade. Unlike the Foundling Hospital, whose appearance projects strongly the presence of an underlying design, the appearance of the Palazzo Rucellai seems to come from one drawn on or applied to the underlying structure. From this design arises an image of the entire façade that appears more like a painted representation than an architectural reconstruction of a classical building.

The appearance of the Rucellai façade is ultimately the result of Alberti's general concept that a work of art closely follow a model. Because Alberti's formulation of this concept proceeded

22

from an interest in painting—the art he considered to be above all others—his particular application of it to architecture was shaped by concerns stemming from his desire to give a "lifelike" appearance to painting. Thus, for Alberti, the fundamental means of achieving the appearance of a building were similar to those to be used in painting. For the painter, Alberti outlined a system of perspective, for the architect, a system of proportions. Both were systems based on mathematical means of relating quantities, of which the ones most preferred by Alberti for architectural proportions were those also used in the musical art of harmonics. Such systems, he believed, were divine in origin and were what gave to the works of Nature their appearance of perfection. Because man himself was a work of Nature, he was innately sensitive to such systems and thus would immediately perceive as perfect any work of art in which such a system was present. Visually, the presence of such a system—but not a description of the system itself—was conveyed to the viewer of either a work of architecture or a painting by lines, planes and angles.

Consequently, to create a work of art in material form—building or painting—became for Alberti a process of first reducing his mental image to lines. He had to visualize the work of art within a network of lines disposed according to a mathematical system over the surface of a plane—either a pictorial one or the face of a building. To think of a work of art in this manner was completely natural for Alberti. When, for example, he wished to adduce an illustration for his description of a fine, metal window grating as being made up of an "infinite number of small holes dispersed in a regular order," he visualized it as being "almost like a painting."[19] Naturally, then, Alberti tended to see the different parts of a building principally in linear terms. In one instance, he even describes such architectural members as capitals, columns, bases, etc., as elements the architect had borrowed from the painter.[20] This way of thinking also leads him to define a row of columns as being only "a wall opened and discontinued in several places."[21] He sees this articulated structure as a flat plane, just as it might appear in a photograph taken at an oblique angle. Such a view represents not only how Alberti visualized his buildings, but also how he wished the observer actually to perceive them. It was through such effects as "the Beholder's eye having a clear and distinct view along the Cornices"[22] that Alberti believed the observer would be led

23

to sense the presence of perfection in the building. From the effects produced by an "exactness of lines and angles" the observer would perceive an image of a building whose every part "conspired to form a beautiful Whole."[23]

If, in the Rucellai façade, Alberti's visual image seems simply to be engraved upon the wall complete with network, in other works of Alberti the image of the building arises from the effects of lines and angles less obviously applied to the structure. In the church of S. Francesco in Rimini[24] (plate 27) Alberti is able through such effects to create the image of a harmoniously ordered, classical building, despite the fact that it actually is composed of two separate and quite different models from Roman architecture. For the façade, Alberti chose as his model the Roman triumphal arch (the walled archways on either side of the door originally were intended to have been deeply recessed niches), while the flanks of the church were designed in imitation of one of the many remaining examples of Roman arcaded structures (plate 28). Although physically the façade and flanks of the church are vastly different in scale and structural implication, visually Alberti threads the two together by the continuous lines of the decorative frieze along the base, the projecting moldings of the pier capitals, and the crowning entablature. By these visual effects Alberti fashioned from the two basically incompatible antique prototypes a screen that has the appearance of being made up of a uniform series of piers and arches. The observer comprehends the perfection of the design because he senses the presence in the building of a system that is holding the two different parts together.

Because Alberti believed that visual effects similar to those produced by the sweeping, uninterrupted sight lines of the Rimini church were the principal means of conveying to the observer a sense of the beauty and perfection of a building, he necessarily considered an architect's primary function to be the arrangement of such effects. To select the mathematical means that was to govern all the parts of the building, to construct a linear network by using this ratio to establish its coordinates, and, finally to work within this network to create the desired visual effects, was for Alberti the essence of the art of building.[25] That this concern with what Alberti calls the "Design," constitutes the whole of the architect's creative act is clearly set forth by Alberti in his architectural treatise. Indeed, the entire organization of his treatise is dependent upon the priority of

"Design" over "Structure" and the complete separation of the two. Proceeding from an initial definition that the "whole art of building consists in the Design and the Structure," Alberti arrives at the assertion that "Design is entirely separate from matter." Structure is the material form given to a building by the hand of the builder. Design is the visual image given to the building by the mind of the architect. Thus, for Alberti, a work of architecture was the result of an application of Design to Structure in which the higher logic of the Design necessarily took precedence over any logical system that might either be inherent or implied by a building's structure. In short, following Alberti's approach, the actual organic structure of a building could be hidden, disguised, or invalidated in order to attain the desired appearance.

In the church at Rimini (plates 27, 28), for example, although the transition between the flank and the front façade is effected structurally through a block of solid wall mass, in the design this transitional unit is given the guise of a pier--an architectural unit that actually functions to create a wall rather than simply being formed from it. Seen as a solid block, this corner of the building merely marks the meeting point of two walls equal in height, whose lower and upper limits are stressed by bands of ornament. Seen as a pier, however, this unit places the entire building within the context of one interpreted as an organic structure. It is suggested that the fabric of the church is created by the working together of individual, architectonic units within an overall, logically coherent system. In the light of this suggestion, however, both flank and front of this church are seen to have a separate and individual structural logic. Thus, the result of disguising the corner of the building as a pier is to invalidate the logic inherent in the actual construction in favor of a "design" logic. Alberti treats the corner in this way in order to enhance the visual effect of the building.

The one element responsible for inviting us to read the corner as a pier is also the one most critical for visually uniting the flanks to the front—the projecting molding that wraps around the corner. Within the nature of the organic system it implies, the molding is only a meaningless, decorative strip applied to the building's surface. Visually, however, its role is clear and direct. By echoing the pier capitals along the flank and responding to a similar motif on the façade, it gives the building the appearance of being made up of a continuous series of uniform arches. By

25

36449

LIBRARY
College of St. Francis
JOLIET, ILL.

continuing the projecting moldings of the flank and façade around the corner, it creates for the beholder a line along which he may receive an unbroken view. To enable him to enjoy such visual effects and so to sense the building's perfection and unity, Alberti has subordinated the structural meaning of the building to the meaning of its design.

Following his work at Florence and Rimini about 1450, Alberti designed only two other major, completely new, buildings[26]– the churches of S. Sebastiano (1460) (plates 24–26), and of S. Andrea (1470), both in Mantua.[27] In the façade design of S. Andrea (plates 30–34), Alberti again used a Roman triumphal arch as his classical model, although he chose a different type from the one he used at Rimini. As Alberti did not need to incorporate an existing structure within the Mantuan church, S. Andrea offers us an example of how Alberti's concept of design controlling structure would be applied under ideal conditions. Apparently, Alberti's first step was the choice of a single, identical motif for the entire building–inside and out. The triumphal arch motif was repeated both in form and size on the façade and the sides of the building–a feature he could not have given to the façade and flanks of the church at Rimini. As a result, Alberti was able to maintain the same scale for those parts of the building which had to be joined together to form its shell. By repeating this motif, Alberti again created a building to be perceived by the observer as made up of a continuous series of arched openings. At S. Andrea, however, the observer's experience is quite different. Unlike the Rimini church where his impression is gained by seeing the exterior of the building, at S. Andrea, where the exterior flanks of the building are not visible, he receives this impression only after entering the church. Accordingly, the visual effects Alberti arranged in the façade were aimed at conveying to the viewer a sense of the continuity between exterior and interior, rather than intended, as at Rimini, to allow the eye to encompass the building block.

To create these effects, Alberti again introduced into the façade continuous sight lines in the form of architectural members whose presence invalidates the structural system implied by other elements. The triumphal arch motif, which in the interior is handled in a manner consistent with the organic structural system it implies, is applied to the façade with certain alterations; each one of which works to produce continuous lines that move the eye of the spectator from the front plane of the

26

façade back into the deep recess of the center porch. Unlike the chapel openings, which are its counterpart in the interior, this central recess is framed by fluted pilasters whose presence both destroys the structural logic implicit in the triumphal arch motif and suggests a scale in conflict with the one suggested by the motif. The fluted pilasters function as parts of a different organic system—a system in which the side arches and central door of the recess are also included. Structurally, these smaller openings of the recess could have been incorporated without conflict into the triumphal arch motif. Visually, however, the architectural members belonging to the system of the recess are the means by which Alberti creates the continuous lines for the transition between the front façade and its development in depth. The strongest visual elements to emphasize the transition between flat and receding planes are the individual entablatures whose structural *raison d'être* depends upon the fluted pilasters. Similarly, the entablature over the center doorway is visually continued across the flat front surface of the façade by being transformed into a molding. Although this molding acts to invalidate the structural logic of the triumphal motif, visually it leads the spectator's eye smoothly from front to back. Like the channeled masonry on the Rucellai façade (plate 16), and the corner pier at Rimini (plates 27, 28), this molding is a tangible record of the linear network within which Alberti envisioned his building.

Although Alberti treats as painterly the architectural members which for the classical architects always retained a functional significance, his interpretation of them does not stem from a misunderstanding of the structural role of such elements. That he appreciated and was familiar with their origin as parts of an articulated structure is clearly evident from the section of his architectural treatise dealing with structure (Books I-III). Here, for example, he describes piers, columns, and all supporting or joining members as the "bones or ribs" of a building and refers to those parts which lie between as "fillers up."[28] Throughout this entire section of his book, Alberti uses anatomical terms to describe the various parts of a building and how they contribute to its structure. Thus, when Alberti uses such elements in a nonfunctional manner he does so deliberately and with full awareness of the illogical structure that may result. This consequence is simply unimportant for Alberti who believes the appearance of a building must be the result of its design, not the result of its structure.

The difference in attitude toward architectural elements as parts of, or references to, an organic structure is what clearly separates the work of Alberti from Brunelleschi. Although the contrast that Brunelleschi maintains between wall surface and articulating elements may make such elements appear to be like the lines of a drawing or painting, they are, in fact, always used in a way that hints at, describes, or underlines, a basic structure seemingly responsible for the building's appearance. That Brunelleschi should visualize a building as a skeletal object was in part a natural result of his work as an engineer. But Brunelleschi's desire to give a structural logic to the building through its visual design seems to have been initiated by the example of such medieval Florentine churches as S. Croce (plate 6), whose design exhibits a similar concern to suggest by applied architectural members the existence of a coherent, underlying constructional system. The feeling for the articulation of the structure, which in Gothic architecture led to each vault rib having a response in a wall member and ultimately to a clustering of each of these members, is a concern shared by Brunelleschi. The difference between the east end of S. Croce and that of S. Lorenzo (plate 7) rests principally in the classical vocabulary that Brunelleschi used to illustrate this similar concern for expressing the underlying structure of the building. In S. Lorenzo, as well as in other buildings, no element of the design is left unsupported. Even the entablature above the arched openings into the east-end chapels which physically is only a part of the wall, is visually given points of support by projecting corbels, as if it were a truly functional spanning member. Thus, for Brunelleschi, the visual image he wished to create through the building's design was governed by the "x-ray" manner in which he himself visualized a building.

Although the difference of approach separating Brunelleschi and Alberti is a critical one, ultimately it is only a difference of means occurring within a common attitude toward the creation of a work of architecture. For regardless of whether an architect visualizes his building as a network of lines drawn on a flat surface, or sees it as a wire skeleton, in either instance his purpose in doing so is the same—to be able to determine the visual effect of the building on the observer. If, in the Rucellai façade (plate 16), Alberti uses an arch in a manner that minimizes its organic function in favor of its visual function as a line, while, on the other hand, Brunelleschi conceives the entire façade of the

Palazzo Pitti (plate 14) in terms of the interlocking role played by the different parts making up an arch, nevertheless, both architects incorporate the round arch within their design for the same reason—its ability to lead the eye of the observer from one part of the design to another. This effect of the round arch is what gave it its appeal to the Renaissance architect. Indeed, Filarete's principal argument for the superiority of the classical arch over the Gothic one rests on its ability to present the viewer a continuous, sweeping line of sight. The pointed arch was less beautiful and less perfect than the round one because, as Filarete states, the eye cannot follow its line without interruption, it must "fix itself for a moment at that point where the arch is pointed."[29] By their common appreciation and use of such visual effects, as well as by their common invention of perspective, Brunelleschi and Alberti are bound together as the creators of a new attitude for the art of building. This attitude was a joint legacy of theirs that all succeeding Renaissance architects were to accept as directing their work and development. From now on, the architecture of the Renaissance was to owe its particular form to the personal resolutions by future architects of the fundamental questions first posed by Brunelleschi and Alberti concerning the relationship between design and structure and between image and meaning.

CHAPTER THREE

To find in the 1460's an architect who not only shared Brunelleschi's and Alberti's new attitude, but who also could create buildings of equal quality, was a difficult goal for the Duke of Urbino to attain. Their few immediate followers working in the "classical style" were either architects who simply imitated the appearance of the new buildings, or were sculptors who simply draped a building in a richly carved garb of antique-like ornament and pictorial relief. Of the latter approach, the triumphal entryway applied to the medieval Castel Nuovo in Naples is a striking example (plates 37, 38). Of the other architects, the two most prominent—Michelozzo and Rossellino—show no sign in their work of understanding what motivated Brunelleschi's and Alberti's designs[30] (plate 29). The one work which most closely resembles Alberti's—the Roman courtyard of the Palazzo Venezia[31] (plate 35)—does so only because its architect faithfully copied the arches and piers of the nearby Colosseum (plate 36), without, however, adjusting them to fit within their new compositional context. Such buildings could not provide a proper setting for the ducal court at Urbino where the visual arts were looked upon as one of man's highest achievements. Compared to its development in painting or sculpture, the new concept of a work of art had yet to become a working reality in architecture. However, the three architects who were to make it so–Francesco di Giorgio, Giuliano da Sangallo, and Donato Bramante–were already beginning to work.

In 1465, however, none of these three men had yet achieved sufficient prominence to attract the Duke's attention.[32] About his final choice, Luciano Laurana, we know little aside from his work for the Duke.[33] But by the tower façade design alone he demonstrates his superiority over the man responsible for the Naples entryway (plates 39, 40). The column, which at Naples is treated only as a stone whose surface is to be carved, is used at Urbino as an object having an inner life. Set free from the mass of decoration that at Naples weighs them down, at Urbino, the superimposed archways seem to grow up the façade of their own accord. From his design of the palace courtyard (plate 41), it seems apparent that Laurana was a follower of Brunelleschi who did not simply repeat his forms but comprehended that their beauty and meaning came from the over-all design. The experience of the Foundling Hospital façade (plate 1) is instantly recalled by the sight of this courtyard, even though their individual elements are different. By a similar use of a darker enclosed space, a flat, light-reflecting wall and a contrast between materials, Laurana, like Brunelleschi, makes a silhouette of the classical elements and thus creates the image of a structural web holding the façade in balance. The entire palace at Urbino gives forth the air of a living, organic structure–one that indeed seems to be an antique building reborn. The Duke must have been quite content with his choice of an architect.

Although Laurana was most likely responsible for the greater part of the palace's design, the realization of it was due primarily to a member of the new generation. About 1475, after Laurana's departure, the Duke's principal architect (the one some contemporary sources credit as the palace's creator) was Francesco di Giorgio from Siena.[34] In executing Laurana's design, Francesco exhibits a concern for the building's skeletal structure that, while rooted in Brunelleschi's approach, goes beyond it in re-

31

cognizing and respecting the structural integrity of the classical architectural members. This concern to distinguish between the parts of a building in relation to their structural implication is particularly evident in Francesco's treatment of the courtyard walls of Urbino at the point where they meet one another (plates 43–45). The joining of two separate series of arch-bearing columns is similar to Alberti's problem at Rimini, but Francesco's solution is quite different. At Urbino, the two sets of round arches are not linked by a line drawn onto the surface, but by an implied line of force moving through the pier; its existence is made apparent by a rear "column" that protrudes from the pier mass. Francesco thinks of the pier as filling in the space which would be present if the two wall arcades were simply to meet head-on, as they do in Michelozzo's courtyard of the Palazzo Medici-Riccardi (plate 42). Wherever in the Urbino palace a column occurs in proximity to a wall mass, its distinctive nature is carefully emphasized. A similar concern governs the design of the nearby church of S. Bernardino (plates 48–50). Here, the column acting as a visible support for the crossing arch is kept free from the wall, raised off the floor onto a pedestal —as if the architect considered it to belong to a system separately inserted into the space defined by the walls.

This sensitivity to the separate structural worlds of the column and wall reflects the importance Francesco and his entire generation attached to the classical system of proportions described by Vitruvius. From this source they learned of the different orders of columns and of their origin in the proportions of the human body.[35] Although the text was not always clear as to the application of this system, it left no room for doubt that in classical architecture the column was the controlling modular unit in a building's design. Accordingly, for these architects, the column and its use seemed to embody the secret of the beauty and perfection of classical architecture, and they sought to determine more precisely the system which had governed its use. Being unaware that the system described by Vitruvius (one born in the completely columnar architecture of Greece) had not always been followed in the Imperial Roman buildings that served them as models, their efforts at investigation only deepened still more the mystery of this anthropomorphic system and further confirmed their belief in its existence.

The method invented by Francesco di Giorgio for the application of this system represents the dilemma encountered by these architects.[36] Although Francesco visualized each part of the building as if it were a part of the human body (he saw the profile of an entablature as a human profile; the façade of a church as the standing figure of a man), he did so within a grid-work of lines—not dissimilar from Alberti's network—whose points of correlation were not necessarily determined by a proportional system based on the human body. Francesco's fascination with the idea of a building resembling a human body probably does not stem solely from Vitruvius, but also from his own work as a painter and sculptor. By it, he is linked to the circle of Florentine artists working with Verrocchio, whose detailed anatomical studies (like those of Leonardo) reflected a recent belief that an artist had to know an object from inside-out to be able to create its image. Seen in the context of this general interest in anatomical structure—human or architectural—Francesco stands in relation to Brunelleschi in the same way the painters of Florence in the 1470's stand to Masaccio. In either instance, the desired visual image had become more related to the actual structure of the object being depicted.

In Francesco's work this interest resulted in the formation not only of a somewhat uneasy, self-conscious alliance between the column and the wall, but of a clear distinction as to whether a motif was used for its decorative or structural qualities. On Urbino's exterior palace façade (plates 46, 47), for example, pilasters are used only as parts of decorative frames for windows or doors, not as elements suggestive of an underlying skeleton or of a design (plates 51–53) applied to a surface. When, at S. Maria del Calcinaio, Francesco employs the pilaster to create an image of a structural frame, he transforms it from an elaborately decorated element into an unfluted, broad member of minimal and severe detailing that appears to project from the wall like an exposed post or beam. As each interior pilaster is repeated on the exterior wall, the "frame" of the Cortona church seems actually to pierce the wall. It appears truly functional, strong enough to stand by itself.

The work of Francesco's Florentine contemporary, Giuliano da Sangallo, follows this same direction. The differences between the interior of Giuliano's church at Prato and his model, the Pazzi Chapel, for example, clearly indicate his concern to turn the image evoked by Brunelleschi's design into one that would appear to emanate from the structure itself (plate 55). Giuliano seeks the same visual effects as Brunelleschi but he works to

33

achieve them within a design that makes the wall mass appear to be governed by the precepts of an organic, structural system. Thus the entablature that moves around the Pazzi Chapel (plate 20), without interruption at points of support, is made to operate at Prato as part of an organic system in which the implied lines of force passing from pilaster to arch are materialized by breaking the entablature. Despite these structural "interruptions," the Prato entablature still works visually to lead the eye smoothly about the building, but here it is achieved by a decorative line confined to the frieze. Similarly, at Prato, Giuliano inserts a drum in place of the dark circle of molding that in the Pazzi Chapel is the only element to separate the pendentives from the dome (plate 21). As a result, the resting dome of the Pazzi Chapel, whose illusion of being suspended comes from the continuous molding, appears in the Prato church to be freely floating.

Although Giuliano's general approach is guided by the same structural interest as Francesco's, his personal style is quite distinct. In contrast to Francesco, whose style bears the same graceful and elegant manner seen in Sienese painting, Giuliano works with a feeling for strong, tactile volumes that reveals his Florentine heritage of Masaccio and Giotto.[37] In the exterior design of Prato (plate 54), for example, Giuliano articulates the structure by an interplay of volumes. Through the design of pilasters and marble incrustations, Giuliano visually brings together the protruding arms of this centrally planned church to suggest a single, volumetric block that at the corners is cut away toward a central core, whose existence is indicated by the square exterior shape of the drum. In turn, the corners of the square core are cut away to expose a cylinder—the dome—which diminishes in a series of similar forms until the center point of the whole block has been revealed. By this orderly sequence of diminishing blocks, Giuliano makes the spectator perceive the exterior of the church as a single, volumetric shape. As he knows it to be a hollow shell, the relationship between the exterior and the interior of the building appears to be absolute.

This delight in manipulating pristine volumes to form a building in which each part will appear to belong to a larger, single whole also underlies Giuliano's work of about 1480 at the villa in Poggio a Cajano (plates 57, 59). The arcade completely surrounding the building initiates an implied volume that sets off the main block of the villa as a separate but related volumetric shape. Each architectural detail serves to emphasize the precision of the visual image of these volumes. Pilasters placed only at the corners of the arcade strengthen the side limits of its plane and clearly mark the point at which it extends beyond the main façade. The absence of any decorative pilasters on the façade keeps it intact as a continuous plane. In a sense, the image set up of the villa as a compact, articulated volume is only a prelude in the spectator's experience. For, by the temple front applied onto the façade (plate 58), and by the projecting stairways (originally straight and directly in line with the limits of the temple front), Giuliano creates an axis that disrupts the isolation of the whole building and pierces the main façade.[38] Because these two elements are distinctly additions to the otherwise un-disturbed block, their visual impact is sufficiently powerful to suggest that the axis passes into the building, a suggestion that anticipates the interior arrangement of an entrance hall leading to the center of the block where a vast, two-story salon runs counter to the axis across the width of the entire building (plates 59, 60). This isolated, central room with its massive barrel vault is the final stop in the sequence of implied volumes Giuliano has arranged for the observer to perceive.

Giuliano's ordering of spatial volumes to produce a free-flowing movement from one unit to another, or between interior and exterior, is a three-dimensional realization of the continuous movement between parts that Alberti and Brunelleschi effected by linear elements. The Brunelleschian image of an underlying design must have conditioned Giuliano to this way of seeing, but his principal sources of inspiration were the massive remains of Roman baths. These vast complexes, whose vaulted halls of varying size and shape were axially organized, served Giuliano as models for his own volumetric architecture at Poggio and particularly for his ideal plans for palaces and villas, such as the one designed in 1488 for the King of Naples (plate 56). Giuliano's ideal was to recreate a Roman building from the ground up, because only in this manner could the volumes inherent in its plan become tangible. But, as Giuliano must have recognized, these volumes also were related to the enormous size of the Imperial buildings and except for the vast salon at Poggio, Giuliano never was to have an opportunity to work on such a scale. His frustration must have been extreme, therefore, when the only one of his patrons, Pope Julius II, who desired and could afford to build in this manner, chose another architect,

Bramante, to realize Giuliano's ideal of constructing a building of the grandeur suggested by the ruins of Imperial Rome.

Immediately upon becoming Pope in 1503, Julius II began the most grandiose building program undertaken in Rome since the time of the Emperors. These architectural works were intended to help create the image of a Papacy equal in grandeur to Imperial Rome. In this role, Julius II was carrying out an ideal already established in the 1450's by Pope Nicholas V's plan to make the church of St. Peter's and the Pope's residence on the *Mons Vaticanus* into an architectural complex rivaling the Imperial palaces on the Palatine Hill whose massive ruins stood as a symbol of the power and magnificence of their builders.[39] The passing of the temporal power from Emperor to Pope was to be expressed architecturally by crowning the Vatican Hill with a similar series of imposing buildings. During the time of Nicholas V, the image by which this meaning was to be conveyed was essentially a symbolic one—a symbol provided by the parallel of the building activity itself rather than by an exact correspondence between the new buildings and the Palatine ruins. However, in the sixteenth century, both patron and architect intended to create this image by actually constructing an architectural complex to rival in size and effect the Imperial remains.

Like the Imperial architects, who by massive substructures and retaining walls, had transformed the natural site of the Palatine Hill into a single architectural monument, Bramante molded the diverse terrain and existing buildings in the Vatican area into an architectonic unity (plates 76–78). Across the Vatican Hill he planned to erect two long porticoes, connecting an already existing villa, the Belvedere, to the Palace itself, thereby creating a vast courtyard out of the sloping terrain. Fountains, terraces, connecting ramps, and an elaborate stairway, were arranged to create a central axis that, from a window in the Pope's apartment, could be seen running without interruption to the curved wall of the distant Exedra[40] (plate 77). For the spectator of such a view, or for the one who saw from afar the lengthy enclosing wall against the skyline, the Pope's new palace must clearly have seemed a reincarnation of antiquity's most famous palace—the enormous structure erected by Nero, whose mile-long porticoes the classical writers had specially noted.

The Belvedere, however, was only one unit in Bramante's gigantic project for a complex that included the rebuilding of St. Peter's[41] (plates 79, 80). Like Giuliano, Bramante took the plan of one of the Imperial Baths as a basis for his overall plan. (In one instance, appropriately, Bramante's project is found sketched onto the back of a plan of the Baths of Diocletian.) Within this complex, however, the church itself was to be built on a central plan of the type hinted at in the Pazzi Chapel, used at Prato by Giuliano, developed as an ideal form in the treatises of Filarete and Francesco, and the subject of numerous variations in the drawings of Leonardo. In each of these instances, the physical structure of the church was conceived by visualizing its plan as a square divided into nine equal parts. The volumetric forms implied by each of these divisions were the source for the architect's design of both the exterior of the building and its interior space. As we have seen, Giuliano maintained these volumes as clear and distinct units within his building.

In Bramante's plan for St. Peter's, however, the volumes implied by these divisions are merged together to create an interior space that simultaneously moves through the block in two directions and around its inside perimeter. Because these two major channels intersect, crosscurrents of movements develop that create an endlessly circling space of such energy that it appears to mount by its own force and, in doing so, to be the agent that has molded the building mass. Within such a building, the spectator would truly receive the same spatial experience that he might receive from being within the Roman baths. But Bramante planned a climax to this experience to surpass that of the towering, vaulted halls of the Baths. For above the crossing piers—the only part of Bramante's plan completed—was to rise a gigantic hemispherical dome (plate 79). The effect of its marble walls and coffered ceiling would have been, as Bramante intended, for the observer to see raised up to a new height the most impressive reminder of Roman glory—the Pantheon.

If, by these two buildings, Bramante fulfilled Julius II's desire to create the image of a Papacy equal in power to the Roman Empire, it was not simply because Bramante had been given the opportunity to work on a monumental scale. Indeed, a major factor underlying Julius II's choice of Bramante as his architect probably had been an earlier building by Bramante—the Tempietto—which, although extremely small in size, seemed to his contemporaries to be the very embodiment of classical building (plate 75). To construct a building that would have a scale as monumental as the Roman ones was not for Bramante—as it had been for Giuliano—an ideal that could be realized only through creating buildings of the same size as the Roman ones, nor was it a process dependent upon taking an actual plan of a Roman building as its point of departure. The interior space of St. Peter's, whose effect would have been the same as that within the Roman Baths, does not result from a plan based on these buildings, nor does the complex of the Belvedere stem from any single Roman plan. Bramante, too, did not depend, as Alberti had, upon taking entire compositional motifs from ancient buildings; he used the classical orders to compose his own motifs, like those in the Belvedere courtyard (plate 76). The careful separation between wall and column that marked Francesco's work is replaced in Bramante's by a bold union that produces the sculptured walls of St. Peter's and the richly modeled surfaces of his Roman palaces. Suddenly, in Bramante's work, buildings appear that seem to be continuations of the Imperial Roman style rather than reinterpretations or copies of it. From now on, architects studying in Rome were to include Bramante's plans and elevations among their drawings after antique models. In Bramante's work his contemporaries saw new types of classical buildings—in their experience of them they detected the same spirit of grandeur and magnificence present in the classical ruins.

Bramante was able to invent buildings whose appearance and effect were to seem the same to his contemporaries as those of ancient Rome because his approach was essentially different from that of other architects. Like Alberti, he conceived a building as he would a painting. But in the same way that the painters of his time no longer sought to convey meaning through an ideal representation of the object but through a more naturalistic one, so Bramante's means of achieving the desired visual effects were different from Alberti's. Perspective, in the hands of Bramante, was not an instrument for achieving an image that the spectator would perceive as beautiful or perfect because of a divinely ordered system, but a means of giving a painted object the illusion of being a real one.

Bramante's own work as a painter of illusionistic façade decorations inclined him to follow the same approach in architecture. In his early work at Milan, painted architectural members are often the means by which Bramante creates the image he desires the building to present to the spectator. The most dramatic example of this approach occurs in the choir of S. Maria presso

S. Satiro (plate 61) which gives the illusion of being a deep barrel-vaulted recess but is in actuality only a shallow, painted relief. But these expressions of an essentially Northern, non-Florentine delight in using perspective to deceive the viewer, are only surface symptoms of the basically different attitude toward the relationship between appearance and reality that underlies Bramante's approach. This attitude, for example, allowed him to follow in his work advice contained in Vitruvius about the application of a proportional system that was not believed, or was misunderstood, by both Alberti and Francesco di Giorgio. The statements by Vitruvius concerning the necessity of taking into account the fallacies of human vision when applying a proportional system could not be accommodated within Alberti's method of creating a building by applying to its structure a design determined within a rigid network established by the proportions themselves. Since, for Alberti, the perfection and beauty of the building rested in this mathematically determined system, it could not be altered to make its presence apparent. The spectator was to sense the presence of this system through visual effects that were achieved by altering the structure to fit the design—not, as Vitruvius advised, by altering the design to create an illusion that the structure contained such a system. Not bound by Alberti's philosophical belief in the divine origin of such proportions, Bramante was free to introduce into his buildings the kind of optical refinements advised by Vitruvius. Their presence in such works as the Tempietto, is singled out for particular comment by contemporary writers.[42]

By his acceptance of these principles, Bramante indicates a new concept of the relationship between the model and the work of art that was responsible for his achievements in Rome. The abrupt change in style that occurs between Bramante's work in Milan and in Rome, for example, is only explicable in terms of this attitude. When in Milan, his personal style was not basically different from that of a contemporary architect like Mauro Coducci, and his buildings (plates 67, 68), such as the east end at S. Maria delle Grazie (plates 62–64), only faintly announce his work in St. Peter's. If Bramante seems to become the Renaissance architect who produces the purest classical building since the time of the ancients, it is because his attitude toward his model—Northern or Roman—was to reproduce its appearance by recreating what he felt to be its visual effect. And the means by which the image would be conveyed became increasingly those of the painter or sculptor. Contrasts between light and dark, or between the tactile sensation of different surfaces, are the effects Bramante desired to create in such buildings as the Roman palaces; the atmospheric qualities of a painting by Leonardo are related to Bramante's feeling for physical space as a tangible element; the plasticity of Michelangelo's sculpture is akin to his design for the exterior of St. Peter's; Raphael's grace of line apparent in the cloister of S. Maria della Pace (plates 72–74), and the same artist's clear arrangement of objects in depth underlies the axial arrangement of the Belvedere (plate 78). In short, Bramante's approach leads to an expressive use of architectural elements in a way that creates for the spectator buildings to be experienced emotionally through the impact of purely visual and tactile qualities.

CHAPTER FOUR

To produce, through the effects of the building's surface and by the quality of the space it enclosed, an emotional impact upon the observer became an increasingly dominant aim of the architects who worked in the years following Bramante's death in 1514. Many of the architects in and around the workshop of Bramante (continued by Raphael and Antonio da Sangallo the Younger) returned to their native cities after the sack of Rome in 1527. Suddenly throughout all of Italy and in other parts of Europe, patrons could find architects trained in the new style. As each architect conceived the ideal of the art of building in terms of creating an emotional experience for the observer the buildings of this time become increasingly characterized as the products of a strong personal style. These diverse, and often very contradictory idioms are resolved, however, by their common origin either directly or indirectly, in the work of Bramante.

The work of these architects is primarily determined by the two means of controlling the relationship of the observer to the building that are implicit in Bramante's work: the manipulation of space and the treatment of surface.

In both these respects, the qualities inherent in Bramante's works tend to be exaggerated in those of his followers. Whether rustication is elegant or severe, or whether the space is continuously moving or completely static, such effects appear in their work in a more dramatic form. The balance between any two extremes that marks Bramante's work is absent.

In the palace designed by Bramante's closest associate, Raphael, the contrast between the rustication of the ground floor and the plain, smooth treatment of the main floor is carried out by a subtle echoing of forms and exchange of recessed and projecting elements (plate 85). The sense of control and balance that results allows each of the two elements to achieve its effect without dominating the design. In the work, however, of architects like Michele Sanmicheli (1484–1559) and Antonio da Sangallo the Elder (1455–1534), some fifteen years later, the balance of contrasts is rejected in favor of stressing the visual effect of one of these qualities. Sanmicheli, for example, in the Palazzo Canossa (plate 87) reduces the plastic elements in the façade to an extremely flat, barely three-dimensional state. The precise channeling of the rustication and the crisply cut moldings about the windows give the façade an air of artificiality that is abruptly countered and enforced by the deep recess of the porch. Sangallo, in turn, in the Palazzo Tarugi (plate 86), has removed any suggestion of a delicately layered wall to create a façade of sculptured mass reminiscent of Bramante's merging of wall and column in St. Peter's.

Giulio Romano's approach is still different, for in the Palazzo del Tè one effect is consciously played off against the other through a carefully arranged series of differently treated walls (plates 90, 92–95). The entirely rusticated, long, low entrance wall (plate 90) is slashed by a series of completely smooth, large pilasters. Within the courtyard (plate 92), the masonry increases in rustication, the pilasters swell into columns, and the frieze projects from the wall. Giulio suggests the force with which this transformation has taken place by disrupting the formerly even pattern of the masonry and by making some of the stones of the frieze appear to have slipped down out of place. Although here the classical model may seem far removed (plate 91), the falling stones of the frieze are simply a reflection of a more romantic attitude toward the timeworn classical ruins. Giulio's courtyard design has its closest parallel in drawings by Giuliano Sangallo where the antique buildings are depicted in an exaggerated state of decay that clearly expresses the new emotional approach which the architect took toward his model. As the spectator continued through the villa toward the garden, he passed into a portico where the heavy, sculptured wall of the previous courtyard has been transposed into a screen of free-standing columns whose distinctive nature is heightened by being grouped in fours and silhouetted against the sky (plate 95). The same columns, however, when seen from the garden side lose their identity as free-standing columns for they become a part of a rhythmic chain, made up of more fragile columns, pilasters, and arches, that stretches across the garden façade (plate 93).

While Giulio's personal style is marked by a conscious striving for emotional effects through deliberate contrast of the different qualities inherent in architectural members, the personal style of Baldassare Peruzzi (1481–1536) is expressed through a consistently elegant and refined handling of all parts of a building. Whether it is the design of a single doorway (plate 96), or of an entire façade (plate 97), Peruzzi's work exhibits a fineness and delicacy of detail that is always reminiscent of a drawing. On the Palazzo Massimi façade, whose gentle curve only exaggerates its flatness, the projecting elements appear as darker pen lines, the window-surrounds on the upper stories as calligraphic ornament, and the columns on the ground floor—by being set into the plane and silhouetted against the darker space—as part of a pattern of light and dark.

In the hands of all the architects of this period, the column becomes an extremely expressive element, whether massed within a small, constricted space, as in the entryway of the Palazzo Farnese (plate 101), or made a part of a coloristic pattern, as in Michelangelo Buonarroti's Laurentian Library (plate 104). In this building, a concern for the separate natures of wall and column receives a sardonic statement, as does the functioning role of all the architectural members. For Michelangelo inserts the columns within the wall, breaks the entablature toward them, and supports them on oversized corbels projecting from the wall. By presenting this reversed arrangement of the orders in a light and dark pattern reminiscent of Brunelleschi and

Sangallo (plates 20, 21, 55), Michelangelo suggests the presence of a structural logic which, by being at the same time denied, makes the effect of the entire design enigmatic. His knowingly disrespectful attitude toward the orders also underlies Michelangelo's invention of the Colossal Order, used for the first time on the façade of the Palazzo dei Conservatori (plates 105–107). In this design the column is once again reduced to a minor supporting role, while the pilaster is blown up to become the major visual element now used to make the façade act as a plane to shape the space of the square, and to make clearly visible the similarity of design that links all three buildings along the Capitol square.

Michelangelo's invention of an element to carry the building design across a large distance, and his use of the façade as a space defining unit, are a part of the development by Bramante's followers of the spatial possibilities inherent in his design for the Belvedere (plate 78). Similar to the way their façade designs represent exaggerations of Bramante's, their dramatic use of space stems from a design that in itself is a balanced, harmonious arrangement of parts. Although upon entering the lower court the spectator was given a focal point to see and approach, the force of that axis nevertheless became diminished simply by being enclosed within a courtyard whose outline, a continuous skyline of the long porticoes, imposed itself on any observer. For the spectator, who could view the courtyard from the window in the Pope's apartment, the balance in Bramante's design would have been even more evident, for the focal point of the Exedra —at the top of the hill—would appear to be on the same level as his own.

However, in Bramante's plan, the implications of oriented space as a means of controlling the observer's experience of the building were quickly realized in the work of his followers. Raphael's design for the Villa Madama, for example (plate 88), seems to have been determined by this principle. Taking advantage of the hillside location, Raphael planned a series of gardens along a central axis leading to the main building block. Moving along this axis, the visitor would encounter a series of separate spatial units, each containing a different kind of garden. When seen from the villa, the gardens and walks would merge into an overall design spreading away as it descended. Although the villa block obviously was a dominant focal point in this design, the terraces and walls surrounding it absorbed its height within a broader silhouette somewhat in the way that Bramante's St. Peter's dome (plate 79) merged within the series of surrounding, smaller units to present a more massive and compact silhouette. In both cases, the result of the design was to reduce the impact of any single element in favor of a harmonious arrangement of the parts.

At the Palazzo del Tè, the sequence of effects was also organized along a central axis cutting through the complex from the entranceway to the semicircular loggia at the end of the garden (plate 94). By this means, Giulio made sure that the series of façades showing the gradual freeing of the column from the wall would ultimately be comprehended as a sequential image. Although the entering spectator at either the Belvedere or at the Palazzo del Tè was able to see from one end of the complex to the other along the central axis, at the Palazzo del Tè he had to move through the building to comprehend its entire form, experiencing in turn each of the units composing the complex. In the middle of the sixteenth century both of these possibilities of organizing a complex were exaggerated to provide an even more dramatic experience for the observer.

At the Villa Giulia, a series of courtyards and their connecting passageways are placed along a central axis (plate 111), but the entrance doors linking them are deliberately obscured and, in the first courtyard, other possible exits are made to seem more "natural" ways of leaving it[43] (plate 112). But only if one discovers or is guided to the passageway on the axis can one enter the elegant fountain court beyond (plate 115). On entering, the visitor was abruptly transplanted from the broad open space of the first courtyard to the top of a crescent stairway that led down into a deep well of contained space (plates 113,114). Within its richly decorated walls, he was surrounded by works of sculpture, flowers, birds, and fountains which he was free to explore down to still another level. If he persisted, he would discover hidden here a small, spiral stairway that led up to the last of the courts, an enclosed garden. In this way, the architects of the Villa Giulia turned it into a building that only gradually revealed its wonders for the observer's discovery.

On a smaller scale, a similar sequence of contrasting spatial experiences was created by Giacomo da Vignola (1507–73) in the Farnese Gardens on the Palatine Hill, whose slope was transformed into an elaborate series of stairs and ramps that led through alternatingly enclosed and open space toward two high pavilions (plate 116). Because the pavilions were not placed parallel to one another, but at an oblique angle, the entire unit had the effect of widening out before the spectator as he mounted the hill. At the same time, however, once the observer had reached the upper level, the angular placement of the two buildings acted to narrow and channel the space lying between them. Gardens like those designed by Vignola became increasingly popular after the mid-sixteenth century, for by using such features as trees, wooden arbors, and garden plots, the architect could provide the patron with a vast complex at less cost than one realized only in constructed buildings (plates 118–121). Extending the plan of such a complex over the surrounding countryside not only brought man-made order to nature, but also had a determining effect on the future character of this type of planning. As the principal building came to be placed more frequently at the top of a hill, with a series of terraces and gardens arranged on the slope, the plan became increasingly open in character and tended to be oriented toward a single culminating point (plates 116, 118, 119). In place of experiencing a progression of separate and enclosed units, the spectator now saw a dramatic, perspective vista unfold before him.

The delight in such a vista toward a single terminal point led to a change in Bramante's axial arrangement of the Belvedere. Michelangelo (1551) and Pirro Ligorio (1563) redesigned the Belvedere Exedra and Palace to create a focal point that would clearly dominate the courtyard (plate 78). A similar approach also underlies Michelangelo's design for the completion of St. Peter's (plates 81, 82). Although he returned to Bramante's original, centrally planned building as a model (plates 79, 80) (after Bramante's death, Raphael and Antonio da Sangallo, the Younger, had altered his plans), Michelangelo conceived of the dome as an object to be perceived as a single focal point, lifted above the body of the church and clearly isolated from any subsidiary accents (plate 83). The same effect was exploited by Vignola in his façade design for the Farnese villa at Caprarola, where no projection disturbed the smooth plane of the wall. As a result, the pentagonal building rises steeply from its base to present a sharp, clear image of a cubic form (plate 110).

The separate effects to be gained through the flat wall and the perspective vista were combined in Giorgio Vasari's design for the Uffizi to produce a building of immediate and strong impact (plate 108). In a sense, the Uffizi is not a building but

46

an ideal city street, down whose narrow length we see a triumphal archway. As such it belongs to city planning, but this art in which the architect would control a vast area encompassing a variety of buildings and objects, was not to develop fully until the Baroque architects worked with more plastic forms to attain a bolder modeling of space. Only Michelangelo, in his plan for the city square at the Capitol (plates 106, 107), prefigures their work. But the flat, precise planes of the palaces he designed to define the space appear almost like stage props brought together to cut off the surrounding space, rather than to mold it, as the more massive Baroque buildings were to do.

Yet, between the Renaissance and the Baroque, there exists the work of another architect that seems like a placid interlude between the dramatic and emotional work of men like Vignola, Michelangelo, or Vasari, and the powerful and theatrical work of men like Francesco Borromini and Giovanni Lorenzo Bernini. The world of Palladio's buildings seems at first sight to be of an earlier time, one in which Alberti might have felt at home. We are back where an abstract, mathematical system of proportions makes its presence felt. Yet Palladio's work, too, is an exaggeration, for the effect of beauty and perfection it conveys is more sensuous than that produced by the work of Alberti or even Bramante.

Within the churches or villas of Palladio space is tangible, like Bramante's, but soft and slowly moving, creating the impression more of light than air. Within the church of Il Redentore (plate 127) continuous lines like those used by Alberti lead the eye smoothly without stop down the nave, around the crossing, and back into the arcade where the curved form gently closes the movement. But in Palladio's work this linear movement is achieved through illusionary devices and thus appears to arise more from the body of the building than from the design. If the clear, precise volumetric forms out of which Palladio's buildings are composed (plates 122, 126), hint of Giuliano da Sangallo's work at Poggio or Prato, their differences point up again the delicate quality of Palladio's work. The Villa Barbaro (plates 121, 123) is built on a plan that suggests a boldly projecting center block, but in elevation the block melds with the wings (to which Palladio has given elements of a larger scale) to create a flat façade held in balance and harmony by the symmetry of its parts. As the spectator advances, the building breaks into separate blocks, but the movement is gradual, the effect restrained.

The serenity and extreme grace of Palladio's very classical-appearing buildings enable them to exert a powerful hold over the observer. This sense of perfection and beauty seems neither to rest merely in the buildings themselves, nor to result simply from their design. Instead, it appears to arise from an image that the buildings provoke of being set within an ideal world of their own. Light and air seem to pass through them as if they were not solid structures (plate 124). They are raised off the earth onto pedestals and their form seems to have determined the space and terrain around them (plates 122, 126). Thus, the Villa Rotonda is not set on a hill, but raised up by it (plate 122). Through all these effects, Palladio has created works which evoke not only the image of a classical building but that of an entire classical world of the kind we experience in the paintings of Nicolas Poussin. Palladio has transferred architecture into the realm of illusion that can only be achieved if every part works to create it.

The illusionistic devices that had hitherto been the servants of making apparent what was real were now to become the masters of making real what was only apparent. It is fitting that Palladio's last work should have been a theater (plate 128), for the Baroque architecture that was to follow was born in the illusionistic world of the theater. The Renaissance attitudes begun in the work of Alberti and Brunelleschi, attitudes toward the building as a work of art and toward the relationship between it and the observer, were fundamentally changed. When this happened (plate 129), a new style was begun.

1. Brunelleschi, Foundling Hospital, Florence, designed 1419. (Third story added later.)

3. Ruins of the "Porticus of Pompey," Rome, c. 285 A.D.
  Anonymous sixteenth-century drawing.

4. Roman Forum, Leptis Magna, 200 A.D.
  Detail of arcade.

5. Brunelleschi, S. Lorenzo, Florence, designed 1418, constructed 1421–25, 1442–46. Nave.

6. S. Croce, Florence, begun 1294. Crossing.

7. S. Lorenzo. Crossing.

8. *Brunelleschi, S. Spirito, Florence, designed 1436. Crossing.*

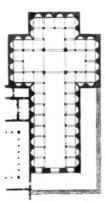

9. S. Spirito. Nave.

10. SS. Apostoli, Florence, End 11th Century.

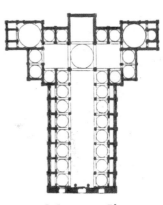

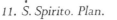

11. S. Spirito. Plan.   12. S. Lorenzo. Plan.

13. *Brunelleschi, Palazzo di Parte Guelfa, Florence, designed c. 1420.*

14. *Brunelleschi, Palazzo Pitti, Florence, designed c. 1440. (Later additions not shown.)*

15. Alberti, Palazzo Rucellai, Florence, 1446–51.

16. Palazzo Rucellai. Detail of façade.

17. Brunelleschi, Pazzi Chapel, S. Croce, Florence, designed c. 1430.

19. Pazzi Chapel. Plan.

18. Old St. Peter's, Rome, early fourth century. Nave Colonnade.
Detail from Renaissance fresco in S. Martino ai Monti, Rome.

20. Pazzi Chapel. Interior.

21. *Pazzi Chapel. View into Dome.*

22. *Brunelleschi, S. Maria degli Angeli, Florence, begun 1434. Plan.*

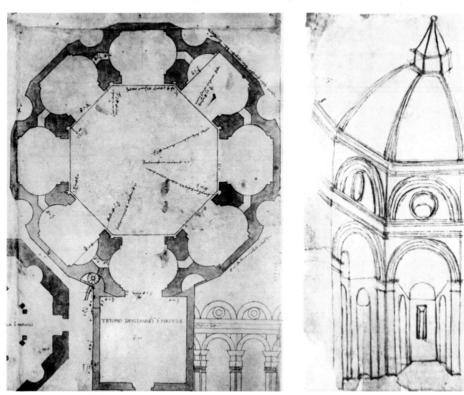

23. *S. Maria degli Angeli. Interior. Anonymous sixteenth-century drawing after Brunelleschi's design.*

24. *Alberti, S. Sebastiano, Mantua, designed 1460, restored 1925.*

25. *S. Sebastiano. Interior.*

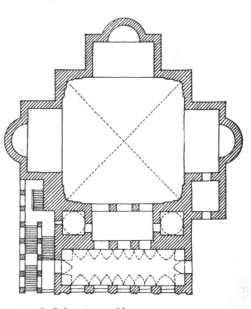

26. *S. Sebastiano. Plan.*

27. *Alberti, S. Francesco (Tempio Malatestiano), Rimini, begun c. 1446.*

28. *S. Francesco. South flank.*

29. *Bernardo Rossellino, Cathedral, Pienza, c. 1460.*

30. *Alberti, S. Andrea, Mantua, designed 1470. Nave wall.*

31. S. Andrea. Exterior.

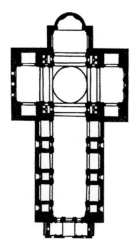

32. S. Andrea. Plan. *33. S. Andrea. Façade elevation.* *34. S. Andrea. Nave wall elevation.*

35. Palazzo Venezia, Rome, c. 1465. Courtyard.

36. Colosseum, Rome, 72 A.D.

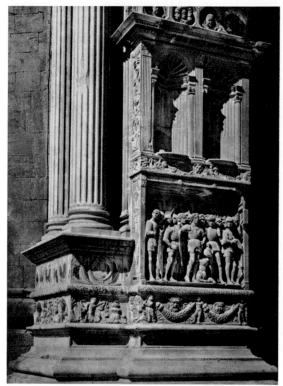

38. *Castel Nuovo. Entry Portal. Detail.*

37. *Castel Nuovo, Naples. Entry Portal, 1453–70.*

39. Luciano Laurana, Palazzo Ducale, Urbino. Tower façade, designed c. 1465.

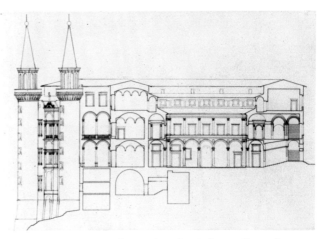

40. Palazzo Ducale, Urbino. Cross-Section.

41. Palazzo Ducale, Urbino. Courtyard, c. 1475.

42. *Michelozzo, Palazzo Medici-Riccardi, Florence, begun 1444. Courtyard. Detail.*

43. *Palazzo Ducale, Urbino. Courtyard, corner pilasters.*

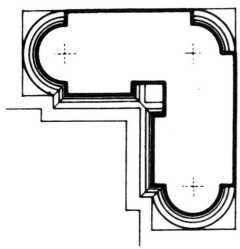

44. *Palazzo Ducale, Urbino. Courtyard. Plan of corner pier.*

45. *Palazzo Ducale, Urbino. Courtyard, corner pier.*

46. *Palazzo Ducale, Urbino. Façade, doorway.*

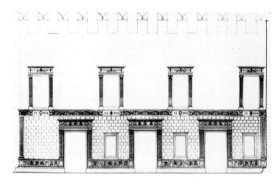

47. *Palazzo Ducale, Façade. Reconstruction by Papini.*

48. Francesco di Giorgio (?), S. Bernardino, near Urbino, c. 1480. Crossing column.

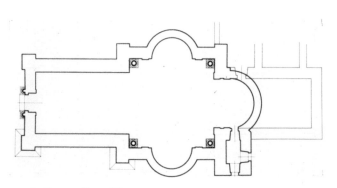

49. S. Bernardino. Plan.

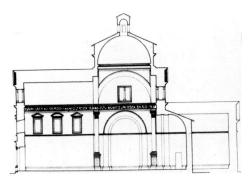

50. S. Bernardino. Cross-Section.

51. Francesco di Giorgio, S. Maria del Calcinaio, near Cortona, designed 1484.

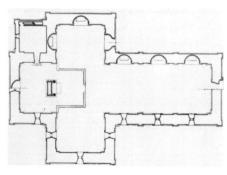

52. S. Maria del Calcinaio. Plan.

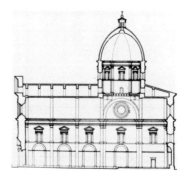

53. S. Maria del Calcinaio. Cross-Section.

54. *Giuliano da Sangallo, S. Maria delle Carceri, Prato, 1485.*

55. *S. Maria delle Carceri. Dome.*

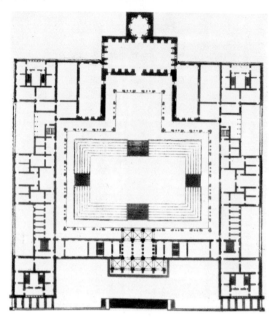

56. *Giuliano da Sangallo, Palace plan for the King of Naples, 1488.*

57. *Giuliano da Sangallo, Villa Medici, Poggio a Cajano, c. 1480.*

58. *Villa Medici, Poggio a Cajano. Entrance Loggia.*

59. *Villa Medici, Poggio a Cajano. Ground Plan.*

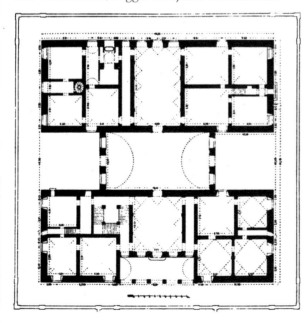

60. Villa Medici, Poggio a Cajano. Central hall.

61. Bramante, S. Maria presso S. Satiro, Milan, c. 1480. Interior.

62. Bramante, S. Maria delle Grazie, Milan. Dome and Choir, begun 1492.

64. *S. Maria delle Grazie. Nave by G. Solari, 1465–90.*

65. *Girolamo da Brescia, S. Giustina, Padua, designed c. 1500.*

66. *Bramante, S. Maria, Abbiategrasso. Portico, 1497.*

67. *Mauro Coducci, Scuola di S. Giovanni Evangelista, Venice. Staircase Hall, 1502–4.*

68. Mauro Coducci, Scuola di S. Marco, Venice, 1485–95.

69. Scuola di S. Marco. Detail.

70. *Palazzo della Cancelleria, Rome, 1486–98.*

71. *Palazzo della Cancelleria. Courtyard.*

72. Bramante, S. Maria della Pace, Rome. Cloister, 1504.

73. S. Maria della Pace. Cloister, detail.

74. S. Maria della Pace. Cloister, pilaster base and pedestal.

75. *Bramante, The Tempietto (S. Pietro in Montorio), Rome, 1502.*

76. *Bramante, Belvedere Court, Vatican, begun 1503.*

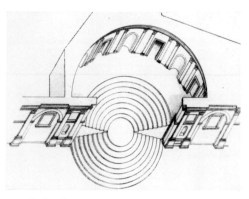

77. *Belvedere Court, Exedra.*
    Reconstruction by Ackerman.

78. *Belvedere Court, Drawing by Dupérac (?), c. 1575.*

79. Bramante, St. Peter's, Vatican, 1506. Elevation drawing from Bramante's Workshop.

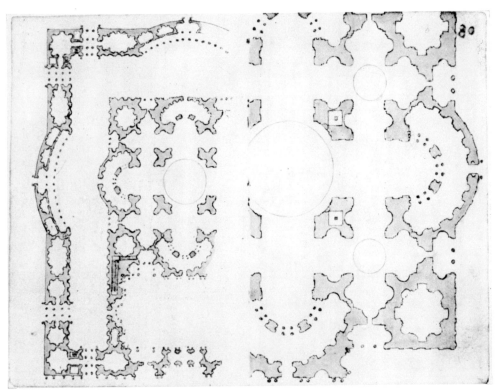

80. Bramante, St. Peter's, 1506. Ground plan from Bramante's Workshop.

81. Michelangelo, St. Peter's. Dome, 1547–61.

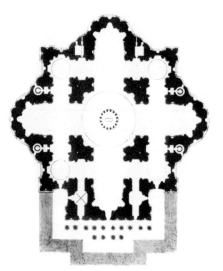

82. Michelangelo, St. Peter's. Plan.
(After engraving by Dupérac, 1569).

83. Drawing by Dupérac (?), c. 1575, after
Michelangelo's Project for St. Peter's.

84. Bramante, Palazzo dei Tribunali, Rome, c. 1512. Reconstruction by Stara.

85. Raphael, Palazzo Vidoni Caffarelli, Rome, c. 1515–20.

88. Raphael, Villa Madama, Rome, 1516–27. Reconstruction by Bafile.

89. Falconetto, Villa Vescovile, Luvigliano (near Padua), c. 1530.

90. Giulio Romano, Palazzo del Tè, Mantua, 1525–35. Entrance Façade.

91. Giuliano da Sangallo. Drawing of Roman Ruin.

92. Palazzo del Tè. Courtyard.

93. Palazzo del Tè. Garden Façade.

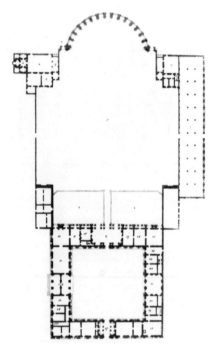

94. Palazzo del Tè. Plan.

95. Palazzo del Tè. Portico.

96. Peruzzi, S. Michele in Bosco, Bologna. Doorway, c. 1525.

97. *Peruzzi, Palazzo Massimi, Rome, begun 1535.*

98. *Palazzo Massimi. Courtyard.*

99. Antonio da Sangallo, the Younger, Palazzo Farnese, Rome, c. 1535. (Top story by Michelangelo, 1548.)

100. Palazzo Farnese. Courtyard. (Top story by Michelangelo, 1548.)

101. *Palazzo Farnese. Entryway.*

103. *Antonio da Sangallo, the
Younger, Palazzo Leroy,
Rome, c. 1523. Detail of
façade.*

102. *Antonio da Sangallo, the Younger, Palazzo
Baldassini, Rome, c. 1520. Entryway.*

104. *Michelangelo, Laurentian Library, Florence. Entry hall, designed c. 1525.*

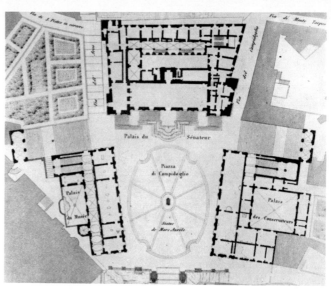

106. The Capitol. Plan.

105. Michelangelo, The Capitol, Rome, 1538-61. Palazzo dei Conservatori. Detail.

107. The Capitol, Palazzo dei Conservatori.

108. *Vasari, Uffizi, Florence, begun 1560.*

109. *Jacopo Sansovino, Library of St. Mark's, Venice, begun 1536.*

110. *Vignola, Villa Farnese, Caprarola, c. 1552.*

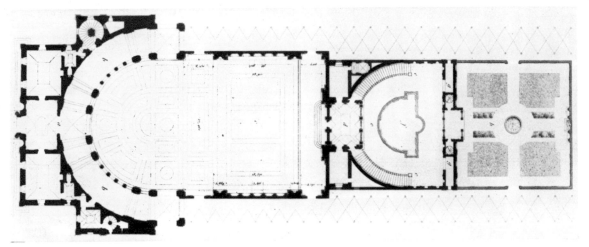

111. Vasari, Vignola, and Ammanati, Villa Giulia, Rome, 1550–55. Plan.

112. Villa Giulia. First courtyard façade.

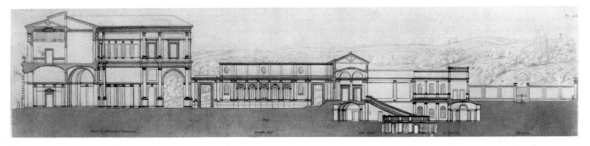

113. Villa Giulia. Longitudinal section.

114. Villa Giulia. View towards second courtyard.

115. Villa Giulia. Second courtyard. Detail of end wall.

116. Vignola, Farnese Gardens, Rome, c. 1560. Destroyed nineteenth century.

117. Pirro Ligorio, Villa d'Este, Tivoli, designed 1549.

118. Vignola (?), Villa Lante, Bagnaia, c. 1560.

119. *Buontalenti, Villa Medici, Pratolino, 1569. Destroyed nineteenth century. (Etching by della Bella.)*

120. *Villa Medici, Pratolino. Plan.*

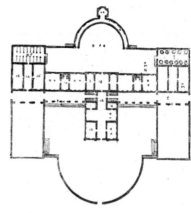

121. *Palladio, Villa Barbaro, Maser, 1566. Plan.*

122. *Palladio, Villa Rotonda, Vicenza, designed c. 1550.*

123. *Villa Barbaro.*

124. *Palladio, Palazzo Chiericati, Vicenza, begun 1550.*

125. *Palazzo Chiericati. Façade detail.*

126. *Palladio, Il Redentore, Venice, 1577–92.*

127. *Il Redentore. Nave.*

128. *Palladio, Teatro Olimpico, Vicenza, 1580–84.*

129. *Giacomo della Porta, Church of the Gesù, Rome. Façade, c. 1575–84.*

NOTES

1. P. Rotondi, *Il Palazzo Ducale di Urbino,* Urbino, 1950, Vol. 1, pp. 109 ff. Notarial document of June 10, 1468, describing search begun probably in 1465 or 1466.

2. E. G. Holt, *A Documentary History of Art,* New York, 1957, Vol. 1, p. 248. As no complete edition of Filarete's treatise is available, all references given are from Holt. Filarete (Antonio Averlino, born c. 1400, died c. 1469) worked most of his life as a sculptor (Florence and Rome), coming to Milan c. 1450, where for the next fourteen years he worked for Duke Francesco Sforza. No buildings by him now exist save a section of the Ospedale Maggiore, a work begun in 1457. Filarete's design was modeled after Brunelleschi's Foundling Hospital but greatly modified in the course of execution to include a rich Gothic ornamentation.

3. The windows above the roof line are a later addition.

4. Masaccio's *Holy Trinity,* c. 1425, S. Maria Novella, Florence, or panels painted by Brunelleschi himself.

5. For a detailed discussion and bibliography of Alberti's and Brunelleschi's systems of perspective see R. Krautheimer, *Lorenzo Ghiberti,* Princeton, 1956, pp. 234 ff., and John White, *The Birth and Rebirth of Pictorial Space,* London, 1957, Chapter VIII.

6. Antonio Manetti, *Vita di Filippo di Ser Brunellesco,* Florence, 1927, pp. 20 ff.; (for English translation see Holt, *op. cit.,* pp. 178 f.).

7. For a discussion of Brunelleschi's panels see R. Krautheimer, *op. cit.,* pp. 234 ff.; White, *op. cit.,* pp. 114 ff.; for Alberti's see L. B. Alberti, *On Painting,* trans. by J. R. Spencer, New Haven, 1956, p. 106, n. 27.

8. Holt, *op cit.,* p. 252.

9. *Ibid.,* p. 248.

10. Letter by Giovanni Dondi quoted by Krautheimer, *op. cit.,* p. 296.

11. In the 1436 dedication to Brunelleschi of the Italian version of his book *On Painting* written in Latin the year previously.

12. Ghiberti had executed three statues here: *St. John the Baptist,* 1414–16; *St. Matthew,* 1419–22; *St. Stephen,* 1425–28. Donatello: *St. Louis,* 1423.

13. *David,* c. 1430–32 (Museo Nazionale, Florence), H. W. Janson, *The Sculpture of Donatello,* Princeton, 1957, Vol. 2, p. 77.

14. See note 4.

15. Described in Manetti, *op. cit.,* pp. 77 ff.

16. Alberti came to Florence from Rome where he had been living probably since c. 1431 or earlier; left Florence for Ferrara, 1436–39; was again in Florence 1439–43; after this date in Rome.

17. Known in extracts during the Middle Ages, but "re-discovered" in 1415. Vitruvius, *On Architecture,* F. Granger, ed., Cambridge, 1931–33.

18. For dating of Alberti's treatise see summary of problem by Krautheimer, *op. cit.,* pp. 268 f., n. 28.

19. L. B. Alberti, *Ten Books on Architecture,* trans. by J. Leoni, London, 1955, p. 157.

20. Alberti, *On Painting,* p. 64.

21. Alberti, *Architecture,* p. 14.

22. *Ibid.,* p. 204.

23. *Ibid.*, p. 195.
24. Alberti's task was to give a classical appearance to the previously existing church. The building remains uncompleted. Alberti had intended to add to the nave a large, domed ending, resembling the Pantheon.
25. Alberti, *Architecture*, pp. l f.
26. For a discussion of Alberti's remodeling of the façade of S. Maria Novella, Florence, c. 1456, see R. Wittkower, *Architectural Principles in the Age of Humanism*, London, 1952, pp. 36 ff.
27. In its present state S. Sebastiano does not reflect either Alberti's original design of c. 1460 or his revised design of c. 1470. Important details of both remain unknown. For a suggested reconstruction, see Wittkower, *op. cit.*, pp. 41 ff.
28. Alberti, *Architecture*, pp. 47 f.
29. Holt, *op. cit.*, Vol. 1, pp. 249 f.
30. Michelozzo di Bartolommeo (1396–1472) worked primarily as a sculptor until c. 1435. Principal architectural works: Palazzo Medici-Riccardi, Florence, begun 1444; SS. Annunziata Tribune, Florence, 1444–55; Portinari Chapel, S. Eustorgio, Milan, begun 1462.

    Bernardo Rossellino (1409–64) worked closely with Alberti (he supervised the construction of the Palazzo Rucellai). Principal architectural works: Pienza, 1460–62 (Cathedral, Palazzo Piccolomini, and other buildings); Siena, 1460–63, Palazzo delle Papesse. His major and perhaps most original work may have been the choir added to St. Peter's by Nicholas V (see note 39) but credit for its design also is given to Alberti.
31. T. Magnuson, *Studies in Roman Quattrocento Architecture*, Stockholm, 1958, pp. 271 ff.
32. Giuliano da Sangallo (born 1445, in Florence) was at this time working in Rome; Francesco di Giorgio (born 1439 in Siena) was active in Siena; while Bramante (born 1444) had probably left his native town of Urbino for the North.
33. For the most recent, as well as reasonable, discussion of Laurana's work at Urbino, see Rotondi, *op. cit., passim.*
34. The much debated question concerning the relative roles of Francesco and Laurana seems to be most reasonably solved in this way.
35. Alberti does not share this enthusiasm for the anthropomorphic origin of columns. Alberti, *Architecture*, pp. 200 f.

115

36. H. Millon, "The Architectural Theory of Francesco di Giorgio," *Art Bulletin,* XL, 1958.

37. Despite Brunelleschi's more plastic use of both column and wall at S. Spirito, tactile volumes, such as found in Giuliano's work, do not seem to me to have been a positive factor for the development of Brunelleschi's personal style. The lantern and aediculae designed as part of the Cathedral Dome probably owe their massive character more to the problem posed by their distance from the viewer than to a sudden interest on Brunelleschi's part in space and mass. Similarly, the central church of S. Maria degli Angeli becomes less of a strong, space-molding structure when envisaged in elevation rather than in ground plan or cross section. Also, the differences between Brunelleschi's design and his Roman "model" point toward a reduction of the interpenetration of mass and space rather than toward a development of this feature. Like Alberti's, Brunelleschi's work remains essentially two-dimensional in concept. A concern for solid and void and for mass and space as expressive elements would seem to be the mark of the new generation of Francesco, Giuliano, and Bramante rather than of a "late style" of Brunelleschi as suggested by Heydenreich. ("Brunelleschi's Spätwerke," *Jahrbuch der preussischen Kunstsammlungen,* LII, 1931.)

38. This effect has been weakened by the vertical axis created through the addition of the curved stairway and clock tower.

39. T. Magnuson, "The Project of Nicholas V for Rebuilding the Borgo Leonino in Rome," *Art Bulletin,* XXXVI, 1954.

40. J. S. Ackerman, *The Cortile del Belvedere,* Vatican, 1954, p. 122.

41. No satisfactory solution to the series of variously attributed drawings for St. Peter's has yet been found. The most recent analysis of the problem can be found in O. H. Förster, *Bramante,* Vienna, 1956, pp. 209 ff. Although the drawings reproduced here (79, 80) are clearly not exact copies of Bramante's design, they probably indicate more accurately than others the nature of the entire project.

42. Such optical refinements are discussed in the edition of Vitruvius (Como, 1521) published by Cesariano, another member of the Milanese Court.

43. John Coolidge was the first to analyze the Villa Giulia in this regard, "The Villa Giulia," *Art Bulletin,* XXV, 1943.

SELECTED BIBLIOGRAPHY

GENERAL

L. B. ALBERTI, *Ten Books on Architecture,* trans. by J. Leoni, London, 1955.

L. B. ALBERTI, *On Painting,* trans. by J. R. Spencer, New Haven, 1956.

W. J. ANDERSON & A. STRATTON, *The Architecture of the Renaissance in Italy,* London, 1927.

J. BAUM, *Baukunst und Dekorative Plastik der Frührenaissance in Italien,* Stuttgart, 1920.

L. BECHERUCCI, *L'architettura italiana del Cinquecento,* Florence, 1936.

J. BURCKHARDT, *Geschichte der Renaissance in Italien,* 5th ed., Esslingen, 1912.

D. FREY, *Architecture of the Renaissance from Brunelleschi to Michel Angelo,* The Hague, 1925.

G. GIOVANNONI, *Saggi sull'architettura del Rinascimento*, 2nd ed., Milan, 1935.

G. GROMART, *L'architecture de la renaissance en Italie*, Paris, 1922.

A. HAUPT, *Renaissance Palaces of Northern Italy and Tuscany*, 3 vols., London, c. 1931.

E. G. HOLT, *A Documentary History of Art*, 2 vols., New York, 1957–58.

W. LOTZ, "Architecture in the Later 16th Century," *College Art Journal*, XVII, 1958.

B. LOWRY, "High Renaissance Architecture," *College Art Journal*, XVII, 1958.

T. MAGNUSON, *Studies in Roman Quattrocento Architecture*, Stockholm, 1958.

A. PALLADIO, *I Quattro libri dell'architettura*, Venice, 1570. (Facsimile edition, Milan, 1945).

N. PEVSNER, "The Architecture of Mannerism," *The Mint*, 1946.

C. RICCI, *L'architettura del Cinquecento in Italia*. Stuttgart, 1928.

G. SEPE, *Rilievi e studi dei Monumenti antichi nel Rinascimento*, Naples, 1939.

C. VON STEGMANN & H. VON GEYMÜLLER, *The Architecture of the Renaissance in Tuscany*, 12 vols., Munich, 1909; English ed., 2 vols., New York, n. d.

A. VENTURI, *Storia dell'arte italiana:* Vol. 8 (Pts. 1 & 2), "L'Architettura del Quattrocento," Milan, 1923; Vol. 11 (Pts. 1–3), "L'architettura del Cinquecento," Milan, 1942.

VITRUVIUS, *On Architecture*, Frank Granger, ed., 2 vols., Cambridge, 1931–33.

H. WILLICH & P. ZUCKER, *Baukunst der Renaissance in Italien*, 2 vols., Potsdam, 1914. (1 vol., Potsdam, 1925.)

R. WITTKOWER, *Architectural Principles in the Age of Humanism*, London, 1952.

R. ZÜRCHER, *Stilprobleme der italienischen Baukunst des Cinquecento*, Basel, 1947.

ARCHITECTS

J. S. ACKERMAN, *The Architecture of Michelangelo*, 2 vols., London, 1961.

C. D'ARCO, *Istoria della Vita e delle Opere di Giulio Pippi Romano*, Mantua, 1838.

G. C. ARGAN, *Brunelleschi*, Milan, 1955.

C. BARONI, *Bramante*, Bergamo, 1941.

F. BURGER, *Die Villen des Andrea Palladio*, Leipzig, 1909.

E. CARLI, *Brunelleschi*, Florence, 1950.

G. CLAUSSE, *Les San Gallo architectes, peintres, sculpteurs, médailleurs, XVe et XVIe siècles*, 3 vols., Paris, 1900–02.

J. COOLIDGE, *Studies on Vignola*, Ph. D. Dissertation, New York University, 1947.

H. FOLNESICS, *Brunelleschi*, Vienna, 1915.

O. H. FÖRSTER, *Bramante*, Vienna, 1956.

O. H. FÖRSTER, "Bramante," *Encyclopedia of World Art*, Vol. 2, New York, 1960.

P. GAZZOLA, *Michele Sanmicheli*, Venice, 1960.

G. GIOVANNONI, *Antonio da Sangallo, Il Giovane*, 2 vols., Rome, 1959.

L. GORI-MONTANELLI, *Brunelleschi e Michelozzo*, Florence, 1957.

F. HARTT, *Giulio Romano*, 2 vols., New Haven, 1958.

L. H. HEYDENREICH, "Brunelleschi's Spätwerke," *Jahrbuch der preussischen Kunstsammlungen*, LII, 1931.

T. HOFMANN, *Raffael in seiner Bedeutung als Architekt*, 4 vols., Zittau, 1900–14.

C. HUELSEN, *Il Libro di Giuliano da Sangallo*, Leipzig-Turin, 1910.

W. KENT, *The Life and Works of Baldassare Peruzzi of Siena*, New York, 1925.

F. KIMBALL, "Luciano Laurano and the 'High Renaissance,'" *Art Bulletin*, X, 1927.

E. LANGENSKIÖLD, *Michele Sanmicheli, The Architect of Verona*, Uppsala, 1938.

O. K. LARSON, "Vasari's Descriptions of Stage Machinery," *Educational Theater Journal*, IX, 1957.

W. LOTZ, *Vignola-Studien*, Würzburg, 1939.

F. MALAGUZZI VALERI, *La Corte di Lodovico il Moro: Bramante e Leonardo*, Vol. 2, Milan, 1915.

(A. MANETTI), *Vita di Filippo di Ser Brunellesco*, Florence, 1927.

G. MARCHINI, *Giuliano da Sangallo*, Florence, 1942.

P.-H. MICHEL, *La Pensée de L. B. Alberti*, Paris, 1930.

R. PANE, *Andrea Palladio*, Turin, 1948.

R. PAPINI, *Francesco di Giorgio, Architetto*, 3 vols., Florence, 1946.

H. PÉE, *Die Palastbauten des Andrea Palladio*, Würzburg, 1941.

A. M. DELLA POZZA, *Palladio*, Vicenza, 1943.

F. D. PRAGER, "Brunelleschi's Inventions and the Renewal of Roman Masonry Work," *Osiris* IX, 1950.

M. SALMI, "Il Palazzo Ducale di Urbino e Francesco di Giorgio," *Studi Artistici Urbinati*, I, 1948.

P. SANPAOLESI, "Brunelleschi," *Encyclopedia of World Art,* Vol. 2, New York, 1960.

L. SCOTT (Mrs. L. E. Baxter), *Filippo di Ser Brunellesco,* London, 1908.

J. A. SYMONDS, *Michelangelo,* 2 vols., London, 1893.

A. S. WELLER, *Francesco di Giorgio, 1439–1501*, Chicago, 1943.

B. ZEVI, "Alberti," *Encyclopedia of World Art,* Vol. 1, New York, 1960.

BUILDINGS

J. S. ACKERMAN, *The Cortile del Belvedere,* Vatican, 1954.

D. COFFIN, *The Villa d'Este at Tivoli,* Princeton, 1960.

J. COOLIDGE, "The Villa Giulia," *Art Bulletin,* XXV, 1943.

W. AND E. PAATZ, *Die Kirchen von Florenz,* Frankfurt/Main, 1940–55.

P. SANPAOLESI, *La cupola di S. M. del Fiore,* Rome, 1941.

P. ROTONDI, *Il Palazzo Ducale di Urbino,* 2 vols., Urbino, 1950.

M. SALMI, *Piero della Francesca e il Palazzo Ducale di Urbino,* Florence, 1945.

H. SIEBENHUENER, *Das Kapitol in Rom,* Munich, 1954.

R. WITTKOWER, "Biblioteca Laurenziana," *Art Bulletin,* XVI, 1934.

INDEX

Numbers in regular roman type refer to text pages; *italic* figures refer to the plates.

SOURCES OF ILLUSTRATION

James Ackerman, *The Cortile del Belvedere* (Vatican, Rome, 1954): 77

Alinari, Rome: 10, 18, 29, 31, 39, 51, 55, 57, 58, 60, 62, 66, 108, 126, 127

Alinari-Anderson, Rome: 14, 35, 37, 38, 64, 70, 85, 97, 98, 109, 110

Foto Aragonzini, Milan: 61

Carlo d'Arco, *Storia della Vita e delle Opere di Giulio Pippi Romano* (Mantova, 1842): 94

Edizioni Artistiche Fiorentini, Venice: 89

Thomas Ashby, *Topographical Study in Rome in 1581* (London, 1916): 78, 83

Mario Bafile, *Il Giardino di Villa Madama* (Rome, 1942): 88

Roloff Beny, *The Thrones of Earth and Heaven* (London, 1958): 4

Biblioteca Laurenziana, Florence: 23

Ted Borsig, New York: 6, 8, 86

Jacob Burckhardt, *Gesammelte Werke II: "Die Baukunst der Renaissance in Italien"*, (Basel, 1955): 11, 12, 32

Encyclopedia of World Art (New York, 1960), Vol. 1: 26

Giovanni Battista Falda, *Le Fontane di Roma* (Rome, 1675–91?): 117

Gabinetto Fotografico Nazionale, Rome: 28, 45, 46, 48, 72, 73, 95, 96, 102, 103

Cristian Huelsen, *Il Libro di Giuliano da Sangallo* (Vatican, 1910): 22, 91

H. P. Kraus, New York: 79, 80

Kunstbibliothek, Berlin: 3

Paul Marie Letarouilly, *The Basilica of St. Peter* (London, 1953): 82

Paul Marie Letarouilly, *Edifices de Rome Moderne II* (Paris, 1856): 106, 111, 113, 116

Georgii K. Loukomski, *Jules Romain* (Paris, 1932): 90

Georgii K. Loukomski, *Les Sangallo* (Paris, 1934): 56

Bates Lowry, Claremont, Calif.: 43, 84

Georgina Masson, *Italian Villas and Palaces* (New York, 1959): 71, 87, 101

Rollie McKenna, New York: 2, 5, 7, 9, 13, 16, 21, 24, 25, 30, 42, 54, 65, 68, 69, 74, 92, 93, 104, 122, 124, 125

Metropolitan Museum of Art, New York; Dick Fund, 1946: 119, 120

Foto Naya, Venice: 67

Andrea Palladio, *I Quattro Libri dell'Architettura* (Venice, 1581): 121

Roberto Papini, *Francesco di Giorgio Architetto*, Vol. III (Firenze, 1946): 40, 44, 47, 49, 50, 52, 53

Paoletti, Milan: 63

Ch. Percier and P. F. L. Fontaine, *Choix des plus célèbres maisons de plaisance de Rome et de ses environs* (Paris, 1809): 118

Carl Martin von Stegmann and Heinrich von Geymüller, *The Architecture of the Renaissance in Tuscany* (New York, 1924): 19, 59

Foto Unione, Rome: 81

Foto Vajenti, Vicenza: 128

Gall. Mus. Vaticano: 76

John B. Vincent, Berkeley, California: 1, 15, 17, 20, 27, 36, 41, 75, 99, 100, 105, 107, 112, 114, 115, 123, 129

Rudolf Wittkower, *Architectural Principles in the Age of Humanism* (London, 1952): 33, 34

127

Printed in photogravure and letterpress by Joh. Enschedé en Zonen, Haarlem, The Netherlands. Set in Romulus with Spectrum display, both faces designed by Jan van Krimpen. Format by William and Caroline Harris.

Renaissance Architecture

by Bates Lowry

Of all the past periods of architectural activity, the era of the Renaissance is the one most closely related to the architecture of our own time. Not only have the beauty and logic of Renaissance palaces and churches attracted the interest of architectural historians over the past sixty years, but the vigor and excitement inherent in the work of the fifteenth- and sixteenth-century architects are closely paralleled in the intense architectural activity of the twentieth century.

During the fifteenth century in Italy men who were trained primarily in the fine arts began to supplant the mason-craftsmen as designers of the new buildings; and these buildings became works of art in their own right, objects of beauty to be appreciated for their own sake. Architecture thus became one of the fine arts; and for the first time since the first century A.D. in Rome, architectural theory came into prominence as a vehicle of expression for man's philosophical ideas and beliefs. Later, after a gradual acceptance of the architecture of classical Rome as the model for a new style, artistic and political ends fused as papal and ducal rulers sought to glorify their states and themselves by recreating the grandeur of Imperial Rome through the erection of

(continued on back flap)